*Government*
*without Passing Laws*

*The University of
North Carolina Press
Chapel Hill*

# Government without Passing Laws

*Congress' Nonstatutory Techniques for Appropriations Control*

by *MICHAEL W. KIRST*

# *Preface*

When the powers and prerogatives of Congress are discussed, the "power of the purse" is usually mentioned as the most formidable control exercised by Congress. Alexander Hamilton referred to it as a "most complete and effective weapon."[1] Despite the fact that the appropriations process is at the heart of the spending power, little analysis has been attempted of a crucial type of appropriations supervision—nonstatutory control operating through hearings, committee reports, floor debates, and informal meetings.

During this century extralegal appropriations techniques have increased markedly in frequency and significance. In 1943 Arthur MacMahon observed that there had been a "significant change of emphasis in the Congressional attitude toward administrative discretion and its control."[2] He asserted that the complex tasks government fulfills in the twentieth century require administrative flexibility, and consequently appropriations control through the detailed character of the statute is in many instances unfeasible. MacMahon concluded: "The weight is no longer on the initial insertion of statutory detail or upon judicial review. Rather the legislative body itself seeks to be continuously a participant in guiding administrative conduct and the exercise of discretion. The cords that Congress now seeks to attach to administrative action are not merely the predrawn 'leading strings of statutes' of which Woodrow Wilson wrote in *Congressional Government.*"[3]

1. Robert Wallace, *Congressional Control of Spending* (Detroit: Wayne State University Press, 1960), p. vii.
2. Arthur W. MacMahon, "Congressional Oversight of Administration: The Power of the Purse," *Political Science Quarterly*, 58 (1943), 162.
3. *Ibid.*, p. 162.

The relative importance of legislative intent was further enhanced by the recommendations of the 1949 Hoover Commission. In accordance with the commission's chief recommendation, the performance budget concept was implemented to make the statute more meaningful and to reduce the number of appropriations accounts (from 2,000 in 1940 to 375 in 1960).[4] Hence, the appropriations committees no longer attempt to supervise the executive by specifying in the act the amount for everything from stationery to the salary of the guards at the Boston Ship Yard. Instead they employ statements in the committee reports and negotiate transfers informally during the year that exert a more flexible but, nevertheless, effective type of oversight.

Through the years the rules prohibiting legislation in an appropriations bill have been refined and many precedents are now established. The appropriations committees are not always content, however, to operate within the spirit of the rules, and therefore, use legislative intent to circumvent points of order that might be made against legislation in their bills. Furthermore, interviews with appropriations committee members reveal a decided preference for nonstatutory devices in many situations where the statute could be employed. As a result of these developments statutory provisos are restricted largely to housekeeping matters with a consequent increase in Congressional control techniques that do not involve the appropriations act.

This study is based on Congressional consideration of six appropriations bills: Labor—Health, Education and Welfare; Public Works; Interior; Agriculture; State Department—USIA; and Defense. The writer analyzed the basic Congressional documents for the period 1953-62: House and Senate Appropriations Committee reports, the hearings before the five subcommittees, and debate on appropriations bills in the *Congressional Record*. The reports were reviewed initially

4. U.S. Congress, Senate Committee on Government Operations, *Financial Management in the Federal Government*, Senate Document No. 11, 87th Congress, 1st Session (Washington: Government Printing Office, 1961), p. 133.

for committee expectations and instructions; second, the hearings were examined, particularly for discussion pertinent to the points identified in the reports; and third, the *Congressional Record* was reviewed for significant and relevant floor debate. A subcommittee demand or desire was followed, wherever possible, to a point of recognizable response by the executive branch.

This study relies on the printed record, and therefore, many instances of off-the-record control are not included. Some important generalizations, however, are derived from interviews that provided insights that could not be gathered from the record.

The interviews were semistructured and averaged forty minutes in length. Certain key questions, all open-ended, were asked of all respondents. The format was kept very flexible, however, in order to allow particular subjects to be explored with individuals best equipped to analyze them. In order to improve rapport with the respondent, notes were not taken but were transcribed immediately after the interview. Where unattributed quotations appear in the text, they are as nearly verbatim as the author's memory permits.

The writer interviewed three members from the House Appropriations Committee and three from the Senate Committee (who served on four different subcommittees). The chief clerks of three Senate subcommittees and three House subcommittees responded freely to all questions and made available the subcommittee mark-up notes. A draft of this manuscript was provided to the Joint Committee on the Organization of Congress and the writer's conclusions were reviewed for their accuracy. Budget officers in all departments involved in the study were also interviewed.

# *Acknowledgments*

The writer is indebted to the many government officials who furnished numerous insights into the importance and operation of appropriations control without passing laws. Although they must remain anonymous, no doubt they will recognize their contributions and statements throughout the study. The same must be said for the members of Congress and their staffs who gave unstintingly of their time.

Without the encouragement and counsel of Arthur Maass, chairman of the Department of Government at Harvard University, the writer would never have completed the study. His assistance was invaluable and his impress is on almost every section. Joseph Cooper of Harvard University played a crucial part in the conceptual framework. A Harvard seminar paper by John Berg provided the data on the Defense Department appropriations and a critique of several hypotheses advanced in this volume. Finally, W. Devier Pearson of the Joint Committee on the Organization of Congress was a most helpful critic. All contributors, however, must be absolved of any responsibility for the contents.

# Contents

*Government*

*without Passing Laws*

# I. *The Proper Role of the*
*Appropriations Committee*

The constitutional powers of the Congress enable it to exercise a considerable degree of control over the administration of laws. Congress can establish the form of executive organization and control appointments. It can limit administrative action by demanding a legislative veto or investigate and audit executive performance. But it is not the intention of this study to analyze the varied aspects of Congressional oversight of administration. The focus here is on the most important oversight technique—the power of the purse.

The House of Representatives' review of both revenue and spending was lodged in the Ways and Means Committee until 1865. From 1865 to 1921 the locus and effectiveness of fiscal control was replete with developments. The burdensome workload of handling both revenue and expenditure bills led to the creation in 1865 of a Committee on Appropriations. The House members, however, did not accept the centralized dominant control of a single Appropriations Committee and from 1879 to 1885 dispersed the purse power to several legislative committees.

The result was a loss of co-ordinated expenditure control and a tendency for the legislative committees to be captives of the departmental clienteles. A major move toward effective oversight occurred in 1920 when a single committee on appropriations was recreated. This House committee like its Senate counterpart has become one of the most powerful committees in the Congress. Our concern is with the various techniques to control the executive that these appropriations committees have developed.

There are several techniques that come under the broad category of statutory appropriations controls. One distinct type is specification of purpose, a technique that is almost self-explanatory. The rationale behind a statutory specification of purpose is to limit administrative discretion. This is accomplished by defining clearly and precisely the purposes for which money is granted.

The use of this technique has a long history dating back to the opposing credos of the Jeffersonians and the Hamiltonians. During Alexander Hamilton's tenure as secretary of the treasury, the annual appropriations acts provided for only a few lump-sum appropriations.[1] For instance, there was one appropriation for the War Department which could be used for anything relating to the military. Hamilton feared that if the Congress could specify the purpose in any form other than a lump sum, it would want to specify purpose for every object "susceptible of definition." Although this overstates Jefferson's position, the victory of the Jeffersonions has meant a continual struggle between the principles of detailed Congressional control of expenditures and executive flexibility. This flexibility includes transfers between appropriations, a practice that violates the Jeffersonian credo.

Adjustment of fund levels is another type of statutory regulation. The ability of Congress to set fund levels and then to reduce them or increase them provides an important control over the general scope of a program. Also when combined with the specification of purpose, the adjustment of fund levels enables the appropriations committee to direct the particular features of a program. For example, the level of funds provided for the first year of the Marshall Plan determined the scope of the program in terms of whether it was to be a sustained recovery program or a much smaller undertaking, resembling a relief operation. The specification of purpose for distinct fund levels within the general amount

1. Arthur Smithies, *The Budgetary Process in the United States* (New York: McGraw-Hill Book Co., 1955), p. 52. Smithies provides a good history of the Jeffersonian triumph. A thorough history of the House Appropriations Committee is included in Richard Fenno, *The Power of the Purse: Appropriations Politics in Congress* (Boston: Little, Brown and Co., 1966), pp. 42-51.

for European Recovery Programs was the key to whether military features were to be stressed in addition to economic recovery.

Since fund levels control the scope of a program, the traditional scholarly view would not favor widespread use of specification of purpose to regulate specific program features. Under their system Congress would control broad policy decisions, and leave the details of administrative management to executive experts.

Limitational and legislative provisions inserted in appropriations bills constitute a third type of statutory regulation. The rules of both Houses forbid legislation in appropriation bills, but provisions are in order which specify that no part or only a fraction of an appropriation may be used for certain purposes. These conditions can be attached to the language that specifies purposes and funds, or they can be included in a concluding section of the bill.

Provisos are used to control either matters of substantive policy or detailed performance. Indeed the appropriations committees immerse themselves in all kinds of details through provisos. For instance, since 1949 a provision has existed in the Independent Office Appropriations Act barring the use of funds to pay anyone engaged in personnel work if the ratio of personnel employees to other employees in the agency exceeds 1 to 135. Provisos appear in all appropriations acts limiting the number of motor vehicles for each department. A much smaller number of provisos have a significant impact on substantive policy and important programs. One such proviso in the Agriculture Department Appropriations Act requires competitive sales of cotton abroad, a policy that the executive branch strongly objected to because of its impact on foreign policy.[2]

The firm legal status of these three types of statutory controls makes them binding on administrators. The American government is foremost a government of laws, and all three

2. House Report (84-303), p. 29. This style of reference will be used throughout: 84 refers to the 84th Congress, and 303 refers to the document number.

controls appear in the appropriations act. A specific clause in the United States Constitution forbids expenditures without appropriations, and the General Accounting Office and the treasury check administrative compliance with statutory restrictions. In short, the appropriations committees rarely encounter any enforcement problems, because statutory techniques are, in effect, self-enforcing.

A second category of appropriations controls does not involve the statute. This category includes the use of appropriation hearings, reports, and debates to control and guide the administration. These aspects of nonstatutory control are often closely related because the reports many times voice discontent or dissatisfaction that arises in the hearings. In the hearings problems are raised, expectations are affirmed, and understandings are reached; and all this is quite apart from what will finally be included in the statute. The committee reports are used to tie down some of the committee's most important expectations or desires and to formalize discontent over previous expectations or understandings that have not been fulfilled. The committee reports are filled with words of guidance, advice, reprimands, and warning. In fact, the appropriations committees now regard the report language to be so important that they will negotiate over language conflicts between the House and Senate.[3] This importance surrounding nonstatutory devices stems from the fact that they are often found in situations in which the appropriations committees wish to influence important policy. Moreover, nonstatutory techniques are ideally suited in many instances for control of administrative management.

The legal status of nonstatutory control has evolved from several court cases. One of the initial cases to consider the legal validity of nonstatutory language was *Wisconsin Railroad v. Chicago*, (257 US 563). The Supreme Court decided that: "Committee reports and explanatory statements of members in charge . . . have been held to be legitimate aid to the

3. See House Hearings on Public Works Appropriations for 1963, Vol. III, p. 24, concerning Upper Colorado River Transmission and Generation of Electricity.

interpretation of a statute where its language is doubtful or obscure. . . . But when taking the act as a whole, the effect of the language used is clear to the court, extraneous aids like this cannot control interpretation. . . . Such aids are only admissible to solve doubt and not to create it."[4]

The Supreme Court in *Ex Parte Collet* (337 US 55, 61) summed up the present court attitude: "The short answer is that there is no need to refer to the legislative history [nonstatutory comments] where the statute is clear."

In a recent application of these court decisions, the General Accounting Office ruled that the administration legally could ignore carefully worded language in a conference report that had been fully debated on the floor of Congress: "Although the statement of the House managers accompanying the conference report may indicate an intent on the part of some members of the House conferees to prohibit the use of the funds in question for implementing the lease purchase contracts, such a provision was not enacted into a law. An inconsistency between the language used in the statement on the part of the House managers accompanying a conference report, and the language of the bill as enacted into law by the Congress, must be resolved in favor of the language in the law."[5]

Thus, nonstatutory controls are not legally binding upon administration. In some cases the administrator may feel "morally bound" to obey the nonstatutory language, but he can decide when he is or is not "morally bound." Nonstatutory devices encompass a "gray area" in Congressional-executive relations, because their force may vary according to particular customs, situations, and personalities.

Compared to nonstatutory, all three statutory techniques are relatively simple in their operation and impact. Some ad-

4. This study will classify nonstatutory controls according to these legal decisions. Accordingly, where the report language clarifies obscure statutory language, the report language will not be considered nonstatutory and consequently will not be included.

5. House Hearings on Public Works Appropriations for 1958 (85-2), pp. 644-45. See also *Pa. R.R. v. International Col. Co.* (230 U.S. 184).

ministrators feel a commitment to obey almost any Congressional directive, even if they violently disagree. To this kind of administrator nonstatutory devices are the embodiment of the legislature's will, and to disobey violates the integrity of the budget.[6] Other administrators believe they are duty-bound to ignore nonstatutory language when it conflicts with their view of the national interest.

Moreover, appropriations committee members themselves do not have uniform expectations concerning the binding nature of nonstatutory techniques. Some House Appropriations Committee members express the view that the executive should always follow the House committee, regardless of the action taken by the Senate committee on the same directive.[7] Other members of the House committee do not share this view. Consequently, various agencies and appropriations subcommittees work out established customs and relationships that may differ from other agencies and subcommittees. All this means that systematic treatment of nonstatutory control is difficult, and there are exceptions to general descriptions and analyses.

The third and final general category of appropriations control involves continuous surveillances and interim supervision after the bill is passed by the Congress. In recent years, more than ever before, legislators and administrators are in constant contact with each other. Appropriations control is more than just holding hearings, issuing reports, and passing a bill once a year. Rather, it is a process of continual direction by the appropriations subcommittees of agencies within its purview. The appropriations committees are not content to leave administrators complete discretion after formal Congressional consideration is completed. While this process does vary among subcommittees and there is little published concerning it, there is enough evidence to suggest that con-

6. Martin Kreisberg, "The Emergency Rubber Project," in *Public Administration and Policy Development: A Case Book* ed. Harold Stein (New York: Harcourt, Brace and Company, 1952), p. 644.

7. This view was expressed by several House Committee members during interviews.

tinuous surveillance is an important technique for appropriations control.

> REPRESENTATIVE ROONEY [D.-N.Y.]: I am one who believes we should keep in close contact with one another so we understand one another's problems.
> MR. ANDRETTA: I agree.
> REPRESENTATIVE ROONEY: You very often get in touch with us during the course of the year when you do not have a budget pending.
> MR. ANDRETTA: Exactly. . . .[8]

Interspersed in the hearings are numerous references to subcommittee guidance through letters, telephone calls, field trips, *ad hoc* committee-agency sessions, and procedures for prior committee notification. The following example illustrates a few of these interim techniques.

> SENATOR BYRD [D.-W.Va.]: Earlier this year in January and February I wrote Dr. McArdle [Director of Forest Service] and expressed interest in an experimental forest. I went to the state [W.Va.] with Dr. Marguir, Director of the Office of Regional Research, and spent several days in West Virginia visiting various counties. I am informed the Forest Service looks with favor on an experimental forest there.[9]

Continuous supervision is also carried out by the staff of the appropriations committees. The staff's function appears to be partly investigative and partly to carry subcommittee instructions directly to executive officials. A good example of staff penetration of an executive agency involves the Joint

8. Aaron B. Wildavsky, *The Politics of the Budgetary Process* (Boston: Little, Brown and Co., 1965), p. 79.
9. Senate Hearings on Interior Appropriations for 1962 (87-1), p. 752. For an example of an interim agency-subcommittees meeting see House Hearings on Interior Appropriations for 1955 (83-2), p. 196. A *Washington Post* article on January 8, 1962, described how letters from members of the Joint Committee on Atomic Energy prodded the Defense Department into continuing experiments on the development of a ramjet engine.

Committee on Atomic Energy: "According to one former staff man, the . . . Senator wanted the Joint Committee on Atomic Energy [staff] professionals to know more about what was going on in the Commission than the Commissioner did! The staff men have accomplished this directive by going directly to the source of information, the Commission's operating personnel. This direct contact has been maintained not only with personnel in Atomic Energy Commission's Washington headquarters, but with field personnel as well."[10]

These instructions may originate in the minds of either subcommittee members or the staff members. The staff can say it is speaking on behalf of the committee, but executive officials indicate they never know whether the staff is acting on its own.

While interim supervision is important, no systematic examination of it is possible on the basis of the printed record. Consequently, the writer prefers not to include a technique in this study which can be analyzed solely through personal interviews and "hearsay evidence."

This brief description of techniques for appropriations control highlights the fact that Congress possesses a range of alternatives to regulate the executive. There is a scale of control ranging from an informal suggestion in the hearings to a drastic slash in fund levels that emasculates a program.

The three types of statutory controls—specification of purpose, adjustment of fund levels, and provisos—appear adequate to control both substantive policy and administrative detail. The statutory techniques have the attribute of stringency, since to deny funds or to direct their use is to control action. These observations give rise to the question of why Congress relies in a great many instances on nonstatutory devices that carry inadequate legal force. The answer to this question will be a prime focus of this study. Our concern here is with the areas of government policy and management

10. Harold Green and Alan Rosenthal, *The Joint Committee of Atomic Energy*, Washington: The George Washington University, 1961, p. 67.

that this range of appropriations oversight techniques should control.

NORMATIVE STANDARDS

Normative standards are needed to evaluate whether non-statutory control is a "good" or "bad" oversight technique. Norms can be derived from a model of the "proper role" of the appropriations committees. If nonstatutory techniques permit the appropriations committees to exercise a type of control contrary to this "proper role," then a negative evaluation is in order. On the other hand, if nonstatutory techniques allow the appropriations committees to better fulfill its "proper role," the evaluation must be favorable.

## The Appropriations Committee and Broad Substantive Policy

The President's budget serves the dual purpose of programing for the future and of reviewing past performance.[11] Since the budget is the agenda of the appropriations committees, these committees are concerned with Congress' role in formulating future policy and in overseeing administrative performance.

The appropriations committees *with the concurrence of the entire Congress* determine broad policy in two ways.[12] First, through their ability to lower (but not increase) expenditure limits set by the legislative committees, the appropriations committees are able to establish fund levels different from those authorized. For example, in 1949 the Banking and Currency Committees, with the approval of both the House and Senate, established a six-year construction goal of 810,000 public houses. While the act provided for 135,000 houses per year, the appropriations committees cut back an-

11. Arthur Smithies in *The Budgetary Process in the United States*, questions the desirability of combining these two purposes in a single budgetary process. Such issues are beyond the scope of this inquiry.
12. Frequently references to powers and prerogatives of the Appropriations Committee will actually apply to the several subcommittees because of the minimal role the full committee plays in legislative oversight.

nual construction to 35,000 units per year. Obviously, the
810,000 goal of the legislative committee was not even approached.[13]

Moreover, the appropriations committees are able to
completely stymie an authorized program by refusing to
appropriate any money.[14] In 1956 Congress passed, on the
recommendation of its banking and currency committees, a
federal flood insurance program that was to be administered
by a Federal Flood Indemnity Administration in the Housing
and Home Finance Agency. Despite serious floods and hurri-
canes, the House and Senate appropriations committees turned
down all expenditures for starting the program and subsequently the FFIA was forced to disband.

Appropriations committees determine broad policy by setting conditions for the spending of appropriated funds. For
programs authorized by legislation that is very general, and
for those authorized over long periods of time so that regular
review by the legislative committees is not required, the appropriations committees become policy committees by directing procedure and performance. An example of this is
provided by Professor David Knapp, who notes that between
1940 and 1950 nine basic changes in agriculture conservation
policy were made through appropriations provisions.[15]

A case can be made against the appropriations committees'
determining broad substantive policy. If the appropriations
committees are able to influence general policy, they can con-
tradict those views and accomplishments of the legislative
committees that previously have been approved by the entire
Congress (and probably the executive). Consequently, there
is a danger that so much power will be centralized in the appropriations committees that the legislative committees will
be relegated to a minor role.

Present procedure places this tremendous power over appropriations in the hands of small subcommittees whose pol-

13. 10 *Congressional Quarterly* 158 (1954).
14. *New York Times*, July 6, 1957.
15. David Knapp, "Congressional Control of Agriculture Conservation Policy," *Political Science Quarterly*, 71 (June, 1956), pp. 257-81.

icy views and orientation may be different from those of a majority in Congress and even perhaps a majority of the full Appropriations Committee.[16] Professor Fenno's intensive study of the House Appropriations Committee disclosed that:

> Hand in hand with the consensus on their primary goal goes a consensus that all of their House prescribed tasks can be fulfilled by superimposing upon them one, single paramount task—to guard the Federal Treasury. Committee members state their goals in essentially negative terms of guardianship—screening requests for money. Checking against ill-advised expenditures, and protecting the taxpayer dollar. . . . Each executive official . . . is seen to be interested in the expansion of his own particular program. To the consensus on the main task of protecting the Treasury is added, therefore, a consensus on the instrumental task of cutting whatever budget estimates are submitted.

Furthermore, Fenno asserts that although the House Appropriations Committee determines substantive policy, it sees itself as making noncontroversial dollars and cents business decisions. "The Committee makes decisions on the same controversial issues as do the committees handling substantive legislation. But a money decision—however vitally it affects national policy—is, or at least seems to be, less directly a policy decision. Since they deal immediately with dollars and cents, it is easy for the members to hold to the idea that they are not dealing with programmatic questions, that theirs is a 'business' rather than a 'policy' committee."[17]

16. With respect to appropriations bills and reports, the full committee rarely changes a subcommittee proposal. See Arthur W. Mac-Mahon, "Congressional Oversight of Administration: The Power of the Purse," *Political Science Quarterly*, 58 (1943), 177.

17. Richard Fenno, "House Appropriations Committee as a Political System," *American Political Science Review*, 56 (1962), 311. Fenno's pioneering study is restricted to the House Appropriations Committee. The writer's impression is that the Senate Appropriations Committee functions more like other Senate committees than the House Appropriations Committee. Senate committee members (and sometimes the chairman) are on legislative committees in addition to their Appro-

Should broad policy decisions in areas such as foreign aid and public welfare be left to a committee whose overriding objective is guarding the treasury, a committee whose members see themselves as making business decisions?

This would not be a problem if the appropriations committees' jurisdiction were limited to supervision of administrative management and if the legislative committees had the sole responsibility for the direction, volume, and range of programs. Furthermore, a differentiation of roles between the two sets of committees—the one concerned with administrative performance, the other with policy—would eliminate the competition and contradictions that currently result from overlapping prerogatives. To achieve such a differentiation, it would probably be necessary to allow the legislative committees to set monetary *ceilings and floors* in the authorizing legislation, because one way in which the appropriations committees determine important policy is, as we have seen, by setting fund levels. Indeed, questions of how much to spend and for what purposes inevitably have policy implications.

The use of authorized ceilings and floors would force the legislative committees to review most programs frequently in order to adjust monetary limits to current requirements. And these frequent investigations and hearings by the legislative committees would of necessity limit the discretion of the Appropriations Committees to determine policy.

In addition, to achieve a differentiation of roles between the two sets of committees, it would be necessary for legislative committees to include many details in the authorizing legislation. Obviously detailed authorizations limit the number of policy decision the appropriations committees can make.

There are, on the other hand, many sound arguments in favor of appropriations' control of broad policy. In fact, most members of Congress appear to favor overlapping com-

---

priations Committee assignment. This may impede the development of distinctive mores and procedures. Personalities may also be a factor because Senator Hayden exerted a different type of influence upon the Senate Appropriations Committee than Representative Cannon did over the House Appropriations Committee.

mittees' responsibility. Congressmen are ambivalent—they want certain programs, but they also want economy. They have institutionalized this ambivalence by having two sets of committees, each with a primary allegiance to one of these perspectives. Through the interaction of the different policy viewpoints, the conflicting goals of Congress are reconciled.

The underlying philosophy of the 1946 Reorganization Act was that the legislative committees should play a key oversight role for existing programs. Appropriations' supervision of broad policy is needed, however, because the legislative committees, for several reasons, cannot and will not do an adequate job. After an intensive survey of the impact of the 1946 Reorganization Act, Professor Joseph Cooper concluded that the act's primary goal of legislative committee oversight has never been realized.[18] In fact, the legislative committees have neither the time nor the inclination to review all programs in depth every two or three years. The time required for consideration of new legislative proposals and reauthorizations is so great that for most programs only a superficial and infrequent review is possible.

Insufficient time is not the sole reason that the legislative committee oversight is inadequate. In some instances, lack of interest or will account for the neglect of an important program. There is a real danger that the legislative committee will identify too closely with the agency and consequently not undertake a critical policy review.[19]

The budget document is an excellent instrument for review of substantive policy, but it is the agenda of the appropriations committees—not the legislative committees. Consequently, if the appropriations committees' power to control broad policy is emasculated, Congress' best instrument for

18. This information is from an unpublished manuscript by Professor Joseph Cooper of Rice University on the impact of the 1946 Legislative Reorganization Act.

19. See Hearings before the House Interstate and Foreign Commerce Committee concerning an Investigation of Regulatory Commissions (86-1), Part 13, pp. 4947-5008, and Hearings before the House Public Works and Resources Subcommittee of the House Government Operations Committee (86-1).

policy oversight—the budget document—is relegated to a review of administrative management.

The case of the National Institutes of Health illustrates these several points. NIH operated for more than ten years without the legislative committee exercising policy oversight. NIH expanded from a $50 million a year to a $1 billion a year agency in the decade of the 1950's, but the legislative committees did not review or direct any appreciable portion of this growth. In 1963 Chairman Harris of the House Interstate and Foreign Commerce Committee admitted that oversight hearings on NIH were long overdue.

> It seems that there is a great concern among many people with respect to some of these programs and apparently nobody keeps up with things and nobody knows just what is going on over-all in that agency important as it is.
>
> As they called to my attention the other day, within a matter of a few years its expenditures have gone from roughly a million dollars to nearly a billion dollars and, as the Chairman of the [Rules] Committee said to me, "You don't know what is going on and why," and I had to frankly concur that I didn't.
>
> It may be our fault, and part of it probably is, for not staying closer to the situation. We are all busy, as you [NIH] are down there. . . .
>
> I think we should have the whole picture laid out in the record and brought together so we will know who is doing what and whether or not it is justified.
>
> You run a very important agency down there.[20]

If the legislative committees are unable to adequately oversee policy developments, and if at the same time appropriations power over broad policy were to be greatly restricted, our vast governmental bureaucracy would not be subject to sufficient popular control. In effect, granting the legislative committees sole power over substantive policy would

20. Transcript of unpublished hearings provided by Representative Oren Harris.

mean that Congressional oversight would be restricted for long periods of time to an annual appropriations review of administrative management.

Furthermore, if the legislative committees are unable to regularly review authorizing legislation, and if at the same time they were to write detailed rather than general regulations into such legislation, the legislative standards for the conduct of government programs could not be modified to meet current conditions or to reflect current Congressional intent.

Finally, it is impossible to circumscribe appropriations control of broad policy without stripping the appropriations committee of its control of expenditures. In practice it is not feasible to separate administrative management from substantive policy. Questions that abstractly and logically appear to be pure management questions in reality do not concern administrative performance alone. Thus, a decision on whether the Fair Labor Standards Act is to be enforced through spot checks or frequent inspection is not simply a management decision, but a decision that goes to the heart of the policy involved in the act.

On balance, the arguments favoring appropriations control of broad policy are more convincing. The assertion that such control centralizes too much power in appropriations sub-committees can be offset by means other than emasculating Congress' control of spending. In areas where the authorizing committees feel the appropriations committees are exercising an overwhelming influence, the legislative committees can increase their use of short-term and detailed authorizations. If the appropriations committees are confronted with an annual review by the legislative committees, they are not likely to make large cuts below the authorized limit. Moreover, the legislative committees are in a stronger position to overrule the appropriations committees on the floor when they are able to point to their own conclusions on the current policy issues.

THE APPROPRIATIONS COMMITTEES AND
ADMINISTRATIVE DETAILS

There is substantial literature devoted to the issue of whether Congress should regulate administrative details. Most writers condemn interference in administrative detail, and maintain that Congressional power over appropriations should be employed to control fiscal policy and determine the broad policy aspects of money issues. George Galloway, for instance, asserts that "Congress must concentrate on the making of broad policies and oversight of their executive, but refrain from intervening in the operating details of administration."[21] By "details," most critics of current Congressional performance mean details of administrative management. They do not argue that Congress should disregard basic data that are required for making broad policy decisions, but they do assert that Congress should determine the ends and leave the details of implementation to the bureaucracy.[22]

Several writers have displayed concern over the appropriations committees' penchant for supervising the details of administrative management because they fear that the committees will exert a parochial or partisan influence.[23] Professor Key observed, "if the representative body attempts to assume the executive function it tends to be a market place where individuals and factions bargain away the national welfare for sectional and parochial gain."[24] Another viewpoint is expressed by Professor Edward Banfield who criticizes appropriations oversight of details because it detracts from the budget as an instrument of planning.[25]

21. George B. Galloway, *Legislative Process in Congress* (New York: Thomas Y. Crowell, 1946), p. 141.
22. James M. Burns, *Congress on Trial: The Legislative Process and the Administrative State* (New York: Gordian Press, Inc., 1946), p. 116.
23. MacMahon, "Congressional Oversight," Vol. 58, p. 161.
24. V. O. Key, "Legislative Control," in *Elements of Public Administration*, ed. F. Morstein Marx (New York: Prentice-Hall, Inc., 1946), p. 339.
25. Edward C. Banfield, "Congress and the Budget: A Planner's Criticism," *American Political Science Review*, 43 (December, 1949), 1217-18.

*The Proper Role of the Appropriations Committee*

Such arguments neglect to discuss the difficulty of drawing a line between substantive policy and administrative detail. The appropriations committees feel that they must supervise administrative particulars, because such particulars often have a crucial impact on policy. The allocation and orientation of personnel, for example, is of vital significance to the development and effectiveness of any program. As Professor Burns has stated, "power over policy-making and policy-executing has been joined in both President and Congress, as a result of the unity and indivisibility of the governing process and the nature of our political system."[26]

Another dilemma inherent in the traditional scholarly view focuses on support for economy on the one hand and, on the other, for noninterference with the details of execution. If appropriations committees eliminate waste, they are carrying out their paramount task of guarding the Federal Treasury. This function, however, cannot in all cases be fulfilled without inspecting details. In 1960 the House Public Works Subcommittee urged the Corps of Engineers to purchase its own dredges because of the high prices charged by outside contractors.[27] While this directive saved a considerable amount of money, the traditional view would maintain it involves the administrative detail and thus should not concern Congress.

In sum, no attempt should be made to rope off particular areas of exclusive functions beyond which the appropriations committees should not go. Nevertheless, some standards are needed for appropriations supervision of administrative details. Specifically, administrative detail should be regulated by the appropriations committees, but the committees should concentrate on the right kind of details that affect broad policy and general administrative performance.[28] Hence, it may not be desirable for the Public Works Subcommittee to supervise recreation facilities for each national park, but it is

26. Burns, *Congress on Trial*, pp. 116-17.
27. House Report (86-1634), p. 21.
28. See Arthur Maass and others, *Design of Water-Resource Systems* (Cambridge: Harvard University Press, 1962), p. 582.

proper for the subcommittees to establish specific standards that apply to all national parks.

## ENTIRE HOUSE CONTROL OF THE
## APPROPRIATIONS COMMITTEES

The unique contribution of the popularly elected Congress is derived largely from the body as a whole rather than from committees with specialized competence and jurisdiction. This unique contribution contains several elements. First, it can contribute to both the administrative and legislative processes because the entire Congress is a lay group. The collective viewpoint of the legislature is unlike that of a bureaucracy of technicians or experts. The legislature can bring to the evaluation of both policy and administrative performance insights and sensitivities "beyond the perception and ken of any expert."[29]

"Within the Committee, respect, deference, and power are earned through subcommittee activity and, hence to a degree through specialization. Specialization is valued further because it is well suited to the task of guarding the Treasury. Only by specializing, Committee members believe, can they unearth the volume of factual information necessary for the intelligent screening of budget requests."[30] Hence, it is to the influence of the entire House rather than that of appropriations committees or subcommittees that we must look for the contribution of the lay mind.[31] This can be provided by machinery to insure that the whole House can, when it wishes, review the actions of the appropriations subcommittees and/or that the subcommittees are in some ways sensitive to the prevailing will of the whole House.

Another unique contribution of a popularly elected legislature is its institutionalization of the "open mind." This institutionalized "open mind," or capacity for change, can en-

29. *Ibid.*, p. 580.
30. Fenno, "House Appropriations Committee as a Political System," p. 316.
31. *Ibid.*

able the executive to see the obvious and can make him do something about it. An open mind is of vital importance in an age of large bureaucracies that tend to resist change—to carry on as they have in the past.

The contribution of the open mind inheres more in the entire legislative body than in its parts. The appropriations subcommittees deal with many of the same issues each year and become deeply involved in the agencies' problems. The overriding norm of economy may weaken further its capacity to effect change.

The legislature's constituency is different from that of the President. The interaction of the presidential and Congressional constituencies provides a more valid refinement of community consensus than would otherwise be the case. Also, the different constituency of the legislature furnishes an enlightened complement to the outlook of the President. The combined constituencies of the several members of an appropriations subcommittee, however, are not necessarily representative of those of the entire House, nor is the membership of any subcommittee representative of that of the whole House. As Professor Fenno demonstrates, legislators from so-called safe districts who are considered "reasonable men" are usually chosen for the Committee.[32] "The optimum bet for the Committee is a member from a sufficiently safe district to permit him freedom of maneuver inside the House without fear of reprisal at the polls. The degree of responsiveness to the House norms which the Committee selectors value may be the product of a safe district as well as an individual temperament."[33]

The House appropriations subcommittees are nonetheless more representative of the whole House than are most of the House legislative committees, and they are more representative of their parent body than the Senate appropriations subcommittees. In the House, the committee chairman determines the subcommittee membership of the majority party,

32. *Ibid.*, 313.
33. *Ibid., passim.*

and the ranking minority member allocates the minority party membership. These two men make sure that committee members who serve on the House subcommittees represent regions that have little stake in the appropriations under their subcommittee's jurisdiction; hence, they are not reluctant to vote substantial reductions.[34] The Senate subcommittees, however, are filled according to individual preferences, supported by seniority and political necessity. Consequently, the Senate subcommittees are not representative of the entire House and usually vote increases in the House allocations. In both cases, but especially in the Senate, some form of full House control of the appropriations committees is necessary to realize an effective consensus between legislature and executive.

In short, the three elements of the legislature's unique contribution to democratic government are derived largely from the qualities of the whole House rather than of its parts.

NORMATIVE STANDARDS FOR THE PROPER ROLE

From the preceding analysis we can posit that the appropriations committees should oversee substantive policy *and* administrative details. Therefore, nonstatutory techniques can be evaluated on the basis of their contribution to effective appropriations control of both policy and performance. Another norm is that the whole House should be able to supervise its parts and that oversight should be carried out as much as possible through the legislature as a single body. Consequently, a key determinant in an evaluation of nonstatutory devices is whether the entire legislative body is able to adequately review and modify committee proposals for nonstatutory regulation.

34. Robert Wallace, *Congressional Control of Spending* (Detroit: Wayne State University Press, 1960), p. 29.

# II. *Interaction of the Stages of the Appropriations Process*

Each of the nine stages of the appropriations process is utilized for nonstatutory control (including four separate floor debates and three reports). In fact, it is possible for a nonstatutory instruction to be initiated or modified to some degree by every stage, and consequently, the final instruction may be a product of just one or at the most even nine stages. It is the administrator's task to analyse Congressional action at several stages before making a decision on what course to follow. As we shall see later, his decision is based partly on Congressional intent and partly on his own goals. In order to understand how nonstatutory guidance works, we must realize at the outset that the technique is much more complicated than a bald statement in one committee report or a paragraph of statutory language. This complexity and ambiguity give rise to delicate problems of enforcement for the subcommittees and of compliance for the administrative agencies.

NONSTATUTORY CONTROL BY APPROPRIATIONS HEARINGS

The main function of subcommittee hearings is usually to provide information upon which subsequent committee action is based.[1] However, interspersed with this investigative function, the appropriations hearings provide a continual opportunity for nonstatutory direction and regulation. The appropriations hearings may be concerned with anything from trivial details to basic policy, so consequently the 1,000 or more pages of hearings per year on each appropriations bill contain

1. George Galloway, *Congress at the Crossroads* (New York: Thomas Y. Crowell, 1946), pp. 247-49.

instances of nonstatutory regulations that concern both pic-
ayune and substantive policy.[2]

As an independent control device, the hearings are usually
confined to unimportant matters—a specific situation in a
particular Congressional district or a minor administrative detail. Administrative actions that have broad significance, or
are controversial, are usually considered in more stages of the
legislative process than the hearings before either the House
or Senate. If a certain matter is mentioned in the report, the
exchanges in the hearings take on a more mandatory character. A report directive indicates that the entire committee
endorsed the course of action advocated by a particular member in the hearings. Because of this nonstatutory controls
that appear solely in the hearings are more difficult to enforce.[3] A possible offset was disclosed by a State Department
official who stated he took careful note of the tone of voice
that the subcommittee member—especially the chairman—used
when he recommended a certain course of action.[4]

The most frequent nonstatutory technique employed in
the hearings involved urging or prodding the executive to

2. Holbert N. Carroll in his book, *The House of Representatives and
Foreign Affairs* (Pittsburgh: University of Pittsburgh Press, 1958) describes the meticulous and detailed manner in which the House subcommittee on State Department appropriations proceeded. His description
could be generalized to apply to all House subcommittees the writer has
observed.

> The subcommittee of five, seven, or more men devoted most
> of its energy to a tedious examination of scores of projects for
> which funds were asked. . . . The members of the subcom-
> mittee commonly behaved like certified public accountants per-
> forming a pre-audit. The language of the subcommittee was more
> often than not the language of mathematics. . . .
> Questions concerning the substance of the policies involved
> arose from time to time. In general, the members of the money
> subcommittee kept their sights low, upon hundreds of pages of
> justification and structural data. They wandered about in the
> forest of goals and objectives concentrating on the trees. (pp.
> 162-63).

The Senate procedure was different and will be examined in Chapter III.

3. See House Hearings on State Department Appropriations for
1963 (87-2), p. 469.

4. This opinion was expressed during interviews.

take a particular course of action. For example, in 1955 the House Agriculture Subcommittee wanted to end feuding in certain states between the Extension Service and the Soil Conservation Service.

> REPRESENTATIVE HORAN [R.-Wash.]: I want to insist, though, and especially in my state that the Extension Service, the Soil Conservation Service, and FHA be counted in this group. . . . We cannot continue to waste our time . . . with this interagency feuding.[5]

On numerous occasions the appropriations hearings are used independently to spur administrative action on the General Accounting Office audit reports. The audits frequently stimulated subcommittee inquiries concerning the validity of various GAO comments. If the GAO's criticisms were correct, the hearings were usually the only legislative stage the committee employed to implement a remedy.[6] A similar procedure was followed to implement "constructive suggestions" advanced by subcommittee members who had recently returned from field trips. In 1961, Senator Ellender (D.-La.) conducted a wide-ranging field survey of the State Department's overseas operations in thirty-eight countries. Accordingly, the 1961 hearings were filled with specific suggestions by Senator Ellender: ". . . [in Germany] you have seven consulates and in each consulate you have a political section and an economic section. Now instead of reporting through Bonn, the consulates make individual reports to Washington, and that means more employees on the Washington level to read and evaluate them. I was in the hopes that you would look into that . . . and come here with a reduction. . . ."[7]

A great deal of the advice and urging pressed on the administration during the hearings is intended to maintain the familiar Congressional stress upon administrative efficiency

5. House Hearings on Agriculture Appropriations for 1955 (83-2), p. 661.
6. See, for instance, House Hearings on State Department Appropriations for 1960 (86-2), p. 99.
7. Senate Hearings on State Department Appropriations for 1962 (87-1), p. 184.

and economy. A good example of such "thumbnail sermons" on economy was provided by Representative Gore (D.-Tenn.) in the 1948 House hearings on the Atomic Energy Commission appropriations. "What I have sought to indicate by my detailed examination of your department is the feeling . . . that as we move forward into a permanent atomic energy program, which in the very nature of the undertaking is expensive, exploratory, and experimental, that, nevertheless, we must diligently undertake to economize and minimize the cost to the people."[8]

This economy theme was dwelt on constantly and at great length in all subcommittees surveyed. Professor Morgan Thomas pointed out that one such effort at moral suasion did not have much impact on bureaucratic behavior, but he contended:

> . . . these urgings probably have a cumulative impact. By pronouncements of this kind, the desires of these powerful legislative units were made explicit, perhaps disturbing some of the complacency characteristic of most bureaucratic processes, sometimes spurring executive officials to better performances. These pressures may be thought of as designed to create an attitudinal change in administration. That is to say, the Congressmen worked to inculcate AEC administration attitudes of increased concern for executive efficiency and managerial regularity.[9]

A different kind of nonstatutory technique employed solely in the hearings consists of verbal agreements or definite assurances given by administrators to legislators. Often a subcommittee member will make a concerted effort to put the administrator on record to the effect that he agrees to follow a certain course of action.

One such case arose when Chairman Ellender of the Sen-

8. House Hearings on Independent Officer Appropriations for 1950 (81-1), p. 1213.

9. Morgan Thomas, *Atomic Energy and Congress* (Ann Arbor: The University of Michigan Press, 1956), p. 209.

ate Public Works Subcommittee became very upset upon discovering that many completed flood control projects were not being properly maintained by the Army Corps of Engineers.

> SEN. ELLENDER: But I want you to assure this committee that the amount of dollars you are now asking for would maintain all of those [projects] that are now constructed. . .
>
> GEN. CASSIDY [Director of Civil Works]: The level in the budget this year will maintain our projects.
>
> SEN. ELLENDER: And it will not increase the backlog? You know the Democrats remain in power. I shall be here for six more years. I do not want you or any of your successors to come here and tell me of any of your backlogs. If you do, there will be a court martial of our own around here.[10]

Such agreements follow the usual pattern of using the hearings *independently* for unimportant matters that concern only a few localities or minor administrative details. The hearings are relegated to a supplementary role, moreover, in situations where the subcommittee feels that there is a definite possibility that the executive disagrees with the committee's stand.

A hearings agreement that involved only a local constituency is reached in this 1959 exchange and is not mentioned in the report.

> SEN. MUNDT [R.-S.D.]: I have been advised in the 1959 revised program you may be neglecting the Thunder Butte School [for Indians].
>
> MR. ERNST [Assistant Secretary of Interior for Public Fund Managements]: Senator, we will go in and look at it and make sure it is proper. . . .
>
> SEN. MUNDT: If there is a need to spend the money, it is there to spend, but I just wanted to make sure that you were in no sense neglecting the Thunder Butte

10. Senate Hearings on Public Works Appropriations for 1962 (87-1), p. 12.

School in South Dakota. If it [additional construction] is needed, you will go ahead and do it?
MR. ERNST: I assure you we will.[11]

In 1955 Chairman Hill (D.-Ala.) of the Senate Labor–Health, Education and Welfare Subcommittee used a hearings agreement to expedite administrative action. The Railroad Retirement Board had not carried out a provision of the Act charging it with the responsibility to conduct research pertaining to disability studies.

MR. KELLY [Chairman, Railroad Retirement Board]: For some time, I guess almost a year, we have been trying to get together the interested parties to hold a meeting. . . .
SEN. HILL: Now is the Board here present agreeable to fixing a date on this matter?
[A date was agreed upon.]
SEN. HILL: If you do not get them on this date you will have to set another one. You have to keep driving this thing through.[12]

There was nothing in the report about the specific date on which the interested parties would meet.

By contrast when the House Agriculture Subcommittee became greatly concerned because it felt the Agriculture Department had refused in previous years to allot a sufficient quantity of surplus food to the school lunch program, it used the report as well as the hearings to convey its instructions. In the 1957 hearings the administration promised that it would increase Agriculture Department support of school lunches. To make sure this pledge would be honored, the subcommittee report said, "In view of the definite assurances of the Department that increased amounts of surplus agricultural commodities will be made available to the school lunch program

11. Senate Hearings on Interior Appropriations for 1960 (86-1), p. 1079.
12. Senate Hearings on Department of Labor–Health, Education and Welfare Appropriations for 1956 (84-2), pp. 893-95.

during the current year, the committee feels the amount proposed is the maximum."[13]

Instances of the hearings as a supplementary nonstatutory technique are more numerous than as an independent technique. The hearings provide the only opportunity for a face-to-face confrontation with administrators. This situation can be utilized to communicate the urgency and depth of the view embodied in a subsequent report directive, because the legislator can vary his tone of voice to impress the administrator. The very fact that a directive is brought up in the hearings makes the report comment more binding. The combined force of the two stages usually results in some executive response.

Chairman Fogarty (D.-R.I.) of the Labor–Health, Education and Welfare Subcommittee frequently used the cumulative impact of the two appropriations stages to stimulate administrative action.

> REP. FOGARTY: Do you mean that you are satisfied with the amount of work that you are doing on this problem of the aged?
>
> MR. PERKINS [Assistant Secretary, HEW]: No, but I think this whole thing has to be put in its perspective with respect to the organization of our Department. . . .
>
> REP. FOGARTY: One thing I know, Mr. Perkins, is that people are demanding that something be done for the aging. In my opinion, it is not a problem that has been with us for years and years, but it is coming upon us because of the increase in life span and because of the progress in medical research.
>
> SEC. FOLSOM [HEW]: We are planning to put out a report to show exactly what is being done.
>
> REP. FOGARTY: I am not satisfied that you are doing enough in this field. I think you can do more.
>
> SEC. FOLSOM: . . . We might have some further suggestions to make to you as we go along on this.
>
> REP. FOGARTY: I hope you do, because I do not think you are doing enough. I think you can do a lot more

13. House Report (84-2148), p. 13.

29

and can make more progress than you have made. We have been discussing this thing for six years.

SEC. FOLSOM: We have made considerable progress, though, in that time.

REP. FOGARTY: It hasn't shown up in the problems I have come across, Mr. Secretary.[14]

This prodding in the hearings was followed up by a report comment, "It is certainly hoped that in another year something substantial, in the way of a program, will be developed" for the aged.[15]

THE COMMITTEE REPORT AS A TECHNIQUE FOR
NONSTATUTORY CONTROL

While each stage of the appropriations process possesses unique possibilities for nonstatutory control, it is the combined effect of all stages that determines the binding nature of a particular nonstatutory policy. Any stage can negate the action of another stage through an offsetting nonstatutory instruction. The silence of any stage, after a nonstatutory directive is included in a previous stage, can diminish the effectiveness of the nonstatutory directive. Recommendations made in the hearings can encompass anything from offhand suggestions that occur to nonexpert legislators to issues that have greatly concerned the entire subcommittee for several years. The action taken by the committee report can transform a suggestion in the hearings to a directive. If a subcommittee re-emphasizes a suggestion in the report, it means the subcommittee will probably take steps to insure agency responsiveness.

MR. YATES [D.-Ill.]: The gentleman [Chairman Fogarty] talks about a paragraph in the report. . . . But has not the gentleman, as is shown by the hearings

14. House Hearings on Labor—Health, Education and Welfare Appropriations for 1957 (84-2), pp. 23-25.
15. 103 *Congressional Record* 3951 (1957). House Report was reprinted in *Congressional Record*.

before the committee, for years been trying to press the Department into taking some action. . . .

MR. FOGARTY: This is the first time we have written anything like this in the report regarding this program. I am pretty sure that they [Department of Health, Education and Welfare] will come up with a program, as they have in connection with report recommendations of this committee in other programs.[16]

Reports accompanying appropriations bills are considered and theoretically approved by the entire House of Representatives.[17] Indeed the report is a subject of floor debate, and amendments are passed by the whole House to offset subcommittee report statements (See Chapter V). As Representative Fogarty observed: "We are not going to permit it [the report directive] to get lost. Once we make a statement in the report we expect them to live up to it because these reports are the reports of Congress."[18]

The reports, however, are a mixture of suggestions, mandates, warnings, precise instructions, and general advice. What renders this maze comprehensible is a uniform pattern of phraseology attached to each objective. The subcommittees consistently use the same words and phrases to differentiate a suggestion from a mandate. Hence, the writer is convinced that the choice of words by a subcommittee is intended to convey the amount of administrative leeway.

Many report comments merely ratify administrative proposals, but when expressing acquiescence to an executive proposal, the language in the report is usually less forceful. On the other hand, when either a House or Senate subcommittee exercises its own initiative or disagrees with the administration's policy, the choice of words in the report is of

16. 102 *Congressional Record* 3951 (1956).

17. Members of the Appropriations Committee and staff men stated they believed the entire House approved the report. Changes can be made in a committee report during the floor consideration by a number of methods that will be considered in a subsequent chapter.

18. 102 *Congressional Record* 3451 (1956). Of course, the House reports' effectiveness can be hindered by actions in the remaining seven stages of the appropriations process.

paramount importance for conveying the intensity of Congressional feeling and the expected response. Obviously, there is no need for a hierarchy of phrases to make statutory controls more or less binding.

Systematic analysis of nonstatutory controls and guidance is hampered by the different relationships and customs evolved over the years by the several subcommittees and administrative agencies. Consequently, generalizations on report phraseology apply to a greater or lesser degree, depending on particular subcommittee-agency relationships. But the evidence supports the hypothesis that in most instances the committees and agencies are using certain verbs as a code rather than a language. There are arbitrary meanings assigned to these verbs which are different from (although not necessarily in contradiction with) those that they carry in everyday formal language.

The phrases a subcommittee inserts in its report are primarily a function of two variables, the first being the extent to which the committee desires mandatory administrative compliance. The requirements for a binding directive are: (a) the subcommittee feels strongly about an issue; (b) the subcommittee believes it possesses the necessary information to prescribe a course of action; (c) the action prescribed by the subcommittee can be identified easily and hence compliance can be accurately checked; (d) the subcommittee does not feel the administrator needs any discretion. The components of the "mandatory variable" are interdependent, and different phrases can include offsetting combinations. For example, the subcommittee can feel strongly about a certain problem but also believe the administrator needs flexibility to solve it. Consequently, the subcommittee would not use mandatory language.

The type of control that the subcommittee wishes to exercise is the second variable that affects the choice of wording in an appropriations report. Appropriations control can involve an increase or decrease in the budget request, an allocation within a requested amount, or an instruction not directly related to a monetary amount. For each of these a special type of phraseology is employed.

The verbs "directs" and "instructs" are customarily used in situations in which a subcommittee wishes to make extra-legal directives obligatory. Failure of the executive to comply with such "instructions" or "directions" means that the committee will renew its pressure and consider possible sanctions.[19] An Interior Department official revealed that his department scrutinizes the report phrases carefully and classifies those with "instructs" or "directs" within a distinct category called "mandate language." In short, the appropriations subcommittee means "do it or else."

"Directs" or "instructs" are normally used to designate specific actions that the subcommittee can identify easily in the hearings the next year. Consequently, these two words allow little or no administrative discretion since the executive is directed or instructed to carry out a distinct action. For example, in 1958 the Labor–Health, Education and Welfare Subcommittee was concerned because the Labor Department had been seriously considering the regulation of wages and hours of migratory farm workers. "On the contrary, the Congress has consistently exempted agriculture from such controls. . . . Therefore, in providing funds for the carrying-out of the BES program, *it is directed* that such funds not be used directly or indirectly to impose regulations relative to wages, hours. . . ."[20]

"Instructs" and "directs" are used to control both changes in the budgeted amounts and procedures or policies with no direct relations to money. "The conferees *direct* that up to $290,000 be used for construction of transmission facilities to serve Bentonville, Arkansas, referred to in the Senate report."[21]

A similar example from the Bureau of Reclamation appropriations: "The Bureau is *instructed* to obligate no general in-

19. The types of sanctions available to an appropriations subcommittee will be analyzed in Chapter IV.
20. Senate Report (86-425), p. 4. Emphasis added.
21. House Report (84-2413), p. 3. Emphasis added.

vestigation funds during the fiscal year 1956 on advance planning for the Trinity River Project."[22]

This example from the Department of Agriculture illustrates the use of "directs" to alter administrative procedure without any consideration of a definite amount of money: "It has come to the attention of the Committee that this organization [Farmers Home Administration] has established two sets of standards for housing loans—one set for counties which are participating in the Rural Development Program, and another set for the other rural counties of the nation. Many of the members of the Committee feel that citizens of other than rural development counties should have the some opportunities, and *directs* the Department to change its practice and procedure to that end."[23]

The terms "earmarks" or "specifically deleted" are considered just as mandatory as "instructs" or "directs" but are used exclusively to control monetary amounts. These phrases fall within the classification of mandate language and permit little, if any, executive discretion. A certain amount of money is specified for a particular activity. "In addition, $6,000 of the funds provided in this bill *should be earmarked* for establishing a market news service on fruits and vegetables at Blythe, California."[24]

An example from the Labor Department appropriation: "The committee goes along with the House recommendation that $1 million be *specifically earmarked* for juvenile delinquency."[25]

An important characteristic of the use of "earmarks" or "specifically deleted" is that they are often employed in situations in which the appropriations subcommittee changes the requested amount. A different phrase is used if a subcommittee wants to ratify an executive budget request. James Kelly, budget officer of Health, Education and Welfare, confirms this: "I cannot think of an instance where Congress ear-

22. House Report (84-747), p. 6. Emphasis added.
23. House Report (86-1592), p. 56. Emphasis added.
24. House Report (86-365), p. 20. Emphasis added.
25. Senate Report (86-1576), p. 27. Emphasis added.

marked funds from those that were requested [in the budget]. They essentially accepted the funds that were requested and have earmarked funds which they have added over and above the request."[26]

Occasionally, the term "earmarks" appears in the report when it refers to provisos inserted in the bill rather than nonstatutory techniques. This fact supports the contention that "earmarks" carries the strongest possible subcommittee connotation. With regard to all four of these mandate words, all persons interviewed in both branches agree that this distinct category does exist. The subcommittee rarely fails to follow through on whether mandate language is being complied with.

Several verbs intended to allow the administrator some degree of discretion constitute another classification of nonstatutory language. Those most frequently used are "expects" and "urges." These verbs are often found in the context of general as opposed to specific activities and are used to control both monetary amounts and situations not directly related to a money amount. Sometimes a subcommittee is not certain that it is feasible for the executive to implement the "expected" action. In short, "expects" or "urges" are often employed to influence situations that inherently require some measure of executive discretion, and hence the subcommittee cannot direct that a specific action be taken.[27] In such situations, the administrator must use his own judgment as to whether it is feasable and appropriate to follow the committee's guidance. For instance, the Senate Report on State Department appropriations for 1957 reads: "The committee was concerned that only $310,000 was requested for trade fairs behind the Iron Curtain. In the opinion of the committee, it *was felt* that much more good could be accomplished if additional funds were utilized for this purpose. Therefore, the

26. House Hearings on Labor—Health, Education and Welfare Appropriations for 1962 (87-1), p. 56.

27. For example, the Senate State Department Appropriations Committee was concerned that violations of Moroccan treaties were not being properly handled. Senate Report (83-1541), p. 4, said, "The committee again *urges* . . . greater diligence in this matter to assure that the rights of our citizens abroad are fully protected." (Emphasis added)

committee *urges* that every effort be made to have more fairs in Russia and the satellite countries . . . and that more than $310,000 be used for this purpose, *if possible*."[28]

Another situation requiring administrative flexibility involved controls over chemical pesticides. "It is *expected* that responsible officials of the two departments—Agriculture and Health, Education, and Welfare—will work together with private interests so that they all can share in the responsibility of establishing . . . standards to be followed in the use of chemicals for agriculture purposes."[29]

The Congressional view of the mandatory nature of "expects" or "urges" is illustrated by a subcommittee clerk: "If the committee says 'expects,' we are willing to listen to good arguments if the administrator cannot implement the directive. If the report says 'directs,' the administrator better comply or he will pay dearly."

Two examples are presented to indicate the context in which "expects" and "urges" are found. ". . . in the majority of the cases there was no increase at all for training grants. For these reasons the committee *would expect* that approximately 40% of the total recommended $10 million increase be devoted to activities promoting the training of manpower."[30] "The Secretary is *urged* to institute a stronger and more thorough review of research programs under this heading [Payments to State Agriculture Extension Services for Research] in order to curtail duplication. . . ."[31]

The administration's acknowledgment of "expects" or "urges" is, in almost all cases at least, an indication that it will seriously consider the report. If "expects" pertains to an expenditure for a particular program, the agency's opening report at the hearings the following year often contains a statement that more or less emphasis is placed on this area, as requested. If the administration decides not to follow "urges," there is usually a prepared statement of reasons for not doing

28. Senate Report (85-303), pp. 9-10. Emphasis added.
29. House Report (88-1592), p. 12. Emphasis added.
30. Senate Report (85-416), p. 14. Emphasis added.
31. House Report (84-303), p. 13. Emphasis added.

so. In order to make a directive more binding in some cases where "expects" gets no action, the subcommittee the next year uses "directs."[32]

The verbs "expects," "urges," "recommends," "desires," and "feels" display in roughly descending order how obligatory a committee comment is intended to be. Although the latter three allow a greater degree of executive discretion than "expects," they do present a specific course of action. They are used to convey instructions that are related or unrelated to a certain amount of budget funds. Like "expects," these expressions are often used in situations in which some flexibility must remain in the hands of the administrator, who then can apply the committee's views in an appropriate context. With regard to research programs conducted by the State Agriculture Extension Services the House Agriculture Subcommittee in 1956 said: "The committee also *feels* this program should be administered in such a manner as to assure that Federal funds are fully matched by the States.[33] The subcommittee did not use "directs" since they realized there may be some research projects not amenable to watching. Another example: "It is the *desire* of the committee that the Bureau of Reclamation and the utility companies . . . enter into a wheeling agreement to the advantage of the Federal Government and the preferred customers."[34] The subcommittee used "nonmandate language" in order to leave the final decision up to the Bureau of Reclamation. This case illustrates offsetting components of the mandatory variable. The subcommittee feels strongly about the issue but believes the administrator must have discretion during the negotiations with the private utilities.

Another distinct group of phrases included: "it is the

32. Congress created a Section 32 fund to provide some measures of price support for commodities not under the regular support program. In House Report (84-303), p. 19, the committee report "urged" the secretary to use Section 32 funds with greater effectiveness and frequency. In Conference Report (86-588), p. 4, the conferees "directed" that the full authorized amount of Section 32 funds be spent.

33. House Report (84-303), p. 13. Emphasis added.

34. Senate Report (87-1097), p. 35. Emphasis added.

present thought of the committee," "the committee has serious doubts," or "the committee is under the impression." Such phrases can be found in areas where the subcommittee does not feel strongly enough or have the information to urge a definite course of action. They are considered by the appropriations committee as least binding. Unlike all other phrases that have been analysed, these terms do not prescribe a definite course of action. They are suggestions advanced for serious executive consideration but can be ignored without fear of any sanction. A typical example of their context: "The committee is also *under the impression* that the entire program of decentralization [for Bonneville Power Administration] should be reviewed and that office consolidations can be made and *possibly* some of the District and Field Offices entirely eliminated."[35]

A State Department budget officer describes his reaction to such phrases this way: "If a report says such practice is 'doubtful,' we erect as many new buildings as we feel we can justify with a good case. If the report says 'directs' or 'expects,' we really cut back on new buildings, or don't build any."

In sum, the phraseology in the reports often plays an important part in revealing the precise attitude of a subcommittee. By manipulating these various phrases and words in its text, the subcommittee distinguishes between instructions it feels are mandatory and recommendations that can be obviated for good reason. If the administrator disagrees with the subcommittee's views, he carefully considers the choice of wording in the report before determining his response. This excerpt contains all the categories of report phrases.

> Two years ago there was not an identifiable program in the Federal Government aimed at meeting the problem of the mentally retarded. As a result of the action of this Committee, $750,000 was *specifically earmarked* for basic research.
> . . . In its action on the appropriation bill for 1957,

35. House Report (83-314), p. 6. Emphasis added.

the Committee *specifically earmarked* a minimum of
$2,505,000 for further work in mental retardation.
. . . It provided $675,000 for a specific research pro-
gram in the field of education, which program the committee had *directed* the Office of Education to formulate. It provided specifically $80,000 for the Children's
Bureau. It provided specifically $1,000,000 under the
appropriations "Grants to States for Maternal and
Child Welfare," and in its report the committee indicated *the desire* that approximately an additional
$1,000,000 be spent from this appropriation if it could
be soundly and efficiently utilized.

. . . The Committee *will expect* that there be no
diminution in efforts in any of the bureaus now working in phases of this program.[36]

## THE APPELLATE FUNCTION OF THE SENATE
## APPROPRIATIONS COMMITTEE

Contrary to the theory of bicameralism, the Senate Appropriations Committee does not attempt to duplicate the work
of its House counterpart. It never reviews the executive
estimates in great detail but provides an appellate body to
which dissatisfied agencies present their complaints on House
decisions.[37] Usually the Senate raises the House-allowed
amounts, and a balance is reached by the conference.[38]

The executive appeals both statutory and nonstatutory actions taken by the House. Thus, there are frequent compromises between the two bodies concerning nonstatutory dollar
earmarks and report comments. This 1956 quotation provides
a typical example of an executive appeal to the Senate:

36. House Report (85-217), pp. 7, 8. Emphasis added. There are
some cases where language used in the reports is so unusual that it is
clearly not a part of any predefined system. See House Report (87-
574), p. 28.

37. Several years ago, Senator Mansfield said efforts will be made to
have parallel appropriations hearings. If this plan is implemented, it
will alter the Senate's role in appropriations. See *Washington Post*,
January 9, 1964, p. A5.

38. This differentiated role leads the writer to believe that the
norms of the House Appropriations Committee discovered by Fenno
are not applicable to the Senate committee.

... The agency [USIA] wishes to call the attention
of the [Senate] committee to the fact that the report
of the House Appropriations Committee contains specific recommendations which, if forced upon the
agency, would severely limit for the first time the Director's operating authority over his program. While
these recommendations do not have the status of legal
limitation on expenditures by the agency of appropriated funds, the effect would be that the agency would
have to give them *appropriate consideration.*

One of these recommendations is that no funds be
used for a non-profit book corporation, for which
$350,000 was requested. This ignores the fact that this
corporation has been most successful in promoting the
publication and distribution of unattributed American
materials in selected countries.

With respect to motion pictures, the House Report
recommends a reduction of almost $1.5 million. . . .

Experience to date proves that changing demands
on the agency require flexibility in the allocation of
funds to the various activities of the agency.[39]

The Senate committee possesses a range of alternative actions in carrying out its appellate function. It is possible to
remain silent on, reinforce, countermand, or modify nonstatutory controls in the House committee report or hearings.
If the Senate disagrees or agrees with the House on nonstatutory controls, this will usually appear in some form in
the Senate report. At times, however, agreement is revealed
during the Senate hearings or floor debate.

The first alternative is simply to take no action on a House
report comment. This does not mean the House report is
nullified, as would be the case with statutory control. If the
Senate chooses not to comment, a House directive still applies but is simply rendered less binding.

Both appropriation committees realize that the administrator can, with considerable justification, point to silence on

39. Senate Hearings on State Department Appropriations for 1956
(84-1), p. 860. Emphasis added.

the Senate side as a reason for disregarding nonstatutory devices. As Senator Mundt, a veteran of four Senate appropriation subcommittees, pointed out:

> . . . the very fact that we did not concur [with House report statements] should be abundant evidence to those who read the RECORD that we are not joining in the language of the House, because with regard to those measures where we did find ourselves "sympatico" with the House, we specifically concurred.
> For instance, on page 2, with regard to ACP, we say in our report:
> "The committee concurs in the House committee's recommendation."
> Our silence certainly does not indicate concurrence. When we concurred, we concurred in print. I want this specifically in the RECORD.[40]

The executive has not been reluctant to utilize Senate report silence for its own ends. In fiscal 1954 the Fish and Wildlife Service did not want to renovate a fish hatchery in Texas, even though the House report had mentioned it:

> SENATOR JOHNSON [D.-Tex.]: But the administrative officials . . . say that since the Senate Committee does not specify Inks Dam Hatchery, and since the [Senate] report provides that the amount is referred to the budget estimate [for hatchery construction] they would conclude in the absence of any further amendment or legislative history . . . the $35,000 for Inks Dam Hatchery was not included. I wish to clarify the point with the distinguished chairman.[41]

During interviews, executive officials agreed that silence on the part of the Senate committee does allow more administrative leeway and makes House directives less effective.

40. 104 *Congressional Record* 6805 (1958). Notice that Senator Mundt's speech is deliberately calculated to provide the Department of Agriculture with a contrary record that could be cited if the department chose to ignore the House report.
41. 100 *Congressional Record* 7695 (1954).

House committee members admit that silence in the Senate report can be considered by the executive and can be used as a reason for ignoring House nonstatutory language. As a senior member of the House committee put it: "From the point of view of the House and its historic preeminence in the appropriations field, I would see no difference if the Senate were silent on a House report statement. If I were sitting downtown in an executive office, I would see the difference."[42]

Administrators point out, however, that they will comply with a House directive in most cases on which the Senate has not taken a stand. Congress' experience with this situation was accurately summed up by Senator Ellender: "I know of language in the House report, which did not appear in a Senate report, being respected, even though the Senate had not passed on it. . . . However, I wish to assure the Senator from Minnesota that during all the time that I have been a member of the Committee on Appropriations— and that has been quite a number of years—whatever has been written in a report . . . usually has been respected by the authority which is called upon to spend the money [regardless of Senate report silence]."[43]

Another Senate alternative is to reinforce the House statement by concurring with it in its report. "The committee [Senate Subcommittee on Agriculture Appropriations] shares the views expressed in the House report that the Secretary of Agriculture . . . should make a greater effort to dispose of Government-owned commodities in world markets and to thereby reduce the cost of storage, interest, and handling changes."[44]

All persons interviewed are in accord that Senate endorse-

42. Administrators feel that they have the greatest discretion in situations like this: the House ratifies a budget request of $10 million with a restriction on its use; the Senate votes $12 million with no restrictions, and the conferees vote $11 million unrestricted. A State Department administrator remarked that they would use the million over the House allowance in any way they wanted.

43. 101 *Congressional Record* 9863 (1955).

44. Senate Report (86-330), p. 12.

ment of House mandate language is necessary to indicate that Congress regards report language as obligatory.

> SEN. CORDON [R.-Ore., Chairman of Interior Sub-committee]: As I understand the practice in connection with appropriations bills, when the House in the report of its committee recommends the earmarking of a certain amount of funds . . . the recommendation is taken as a directive by the administrative agency, *insofar as this can be done.*
>
> I understand further that if the Senate, acting upon the same bill and the same item joins with the House in such a recommendation, generally speaking, the executive department will deem that to be an *absolute mandate. . . .*
>
> [If the Senate report were silent on a House directive] . . . It was our view that under those circumstances the Department was at full liberty to follow the direction of the House . . . or if it found the exigencies of the occasion to be such that it could not do so, it was *not absolutely bound to do it.*[45]

A Senate subcommittee sometimes includes language in its report that is calculated to countermand the House report. Almost every year the House State Department Subcommittee attempted to earmark specific uses for the State Department's "Salaries and Expenses" appropriation. The department invariably appealed to the Senate on the basis that these earmarks hinder flexibility in American diplomacy. Consequently, the Senate report language offset the House comments. "The Senate committee intends that the State Department utilize the total amount recommended for salaries and expenses to provide what in their judgement is the most essential and desirable to accomplish the missions of the State Department."[46]

Since the conference report does not mention the obvious conflict, the contradictory report instructions are never compromised. This is another situation that could never arise

45. 100 *Congressional Record* 7695 (1954). Emphasis added.
46. Senate Report (85-303), p. 3.

if the statute were involved. The conference would take some action to break the deadlock over statutory language.

The Senate subcommittee is fully aware that   it will countermand House nonstatutory instructions, as is evidenced by this statement of Senator Knowland (R.-Calif.): "Mr. Chairman, I merely want to direct the attention of the committee to some language which appears in the House Committee Report, that I think we will need to give some attention to, to counteract this."[47]

Agency reactions to such deadlocks are not uniform. Interviews with department officials reveal that the State, Agriculture, and Interior Departments take their choice between conflicting reports or ignore both if neither is satisfactory.[48] For instance, in the State Department "Salaries and Expenses" case, the executive followed the recommendation of the Senate subcommittee which allows administrative flexibility. In this situation the House subcommittee could sanction the State Department without being once again offset by the Senate.

In a conflict relating to the Army Corps of Engineers, subcommittee members indicate that they expect negotiations between the two subcommittees and the Corps to resolve the differences. The established procedure begins by the Corps contacting the staff of both subcommittees and requesting a meeting or exchange of letters to reach agreement.[49] Through these informal channels a compromise on directives to the Corps of Engineers is usually worked out. This dissimilarity in agency reaction highlights the fact that the subcommittees operate differently with nonstatutory techniques.

The fourth and final type of impact that the Senate report may have on a House directive is to modify the substance of the instruction rather than its binding nature. For

47. Senate Subcommittee Hearings on State Department Appropriations for 1955 (84-1), p. 1265.

48. Interviews with Congressional employees brought out the same conclusion.

49. This information was given by Army Corps of Engineers employees.

instance, the 1953 Senate Report stated: "In general, the Senate Committee is in agreement with the following Statement in the House Report: 'No land is to be taken by the Park Service through the condemnation procedure.' However, the committee does not feel this provision should apply to the Independence, Pennsylvania project and the committee specifically exempts this project from the statement.[50]

### FLOOR CONSIDERATION OF NONSTATUTORY CONTROLS

The prime importance of the floor debates stems from the opportunity members have to consider and alter recommendations of the powerful appropriations committee. Floor debate on nonstatutory devices is initiated, for the most part, by members who do not serve on the appropriations committee but who have a keen interest in certain directives. The floor debate is carefully read by the agencies because legislators employ it to make a record either for or against a committee action. The most significant feature of floor consideration is the extent to which members are able to clarify, modify, reinforce, or initiate nonstatutory controls.

A majority of the questions raised during the debate concern clarification of a particular report comment. Statements inserted in the committee report are not as carefully worded as provisos in the act. The interplay of the House and Senate upon a directive confuses many legislators not schooled in the subtle meaning of "mandate language," Senate silence, etc. Usually the ultimate objective of the request for clarification is a definite statement by a subcommittee chairman that money for the home district is included. Since the subcommittee chairman is in charge of the bill, most of the questions are addressed to him.

For example, in 1954 Representative Engle (D.-Calif.) inquired of Chairman Jensen (R.-Iowa) of the Interior Subcommittee if language in the committee report struck all money for the Trinity River project or just money for con-

50. Senate Report (83-445), p. 2.

struction. Jensen assured Engle that funds were not disallowed for investigation and planning.

> REP. ENGLE: I was afraid that the language on page 10 of the report would preclude the use of any funds whatever for the Trinity River project for any purpose.[51]

Sometimes floor colloquies add nonstatutory controls through clarification of the committee's intent. For example, Senator Morse (D.-Ore.) complained that the Interior Subcommittee had not specified the location in which increased funds for archaeological investigations were to be used:

> SEN. MORSE: It should be made clear in the legislative record—I think this colloquy will help in the legislative history; that is why I am engaging in it—that it is the intention of the Senate that the National Park Service shall look first [in its archaeological investigations] to the sites which are to be flooded. There is only one in my state.
>
> SEN. HAYDEN [Chairman of Interior Subcommittee]: That is the distinct understanding with which I am undertaking to make this agreement.
>
> SEN. BRIDGES [ranking member]: Having made such a record, I believe we can obtain the objectives we seek.[52]

Often a question, which appears to be a simple request for clarification, is actually an attempt to restrict the application of nonstatutory language to particular circumstances. The questioner hopes to establish a floor record that can be used to modify a report comment in a manner favorable to him. A good example of this may be found in the 1961 Senate Agriculture Subcommittee's insertion of report language requesting the Agriculture Department to distribute farm surpluses "more equitably" among its warehouses.

51. 100 *Congressional Record* 4622 (1954). For a lengthy clarification of a report directive, see 103 *Congressional Record* 13978 (1957) concerning the Seneca Indians.

52. 102 *Congressional Record* 6732 (1956).

SEN. MUNDT: I have received a great many inquiries from Senators who were interested in the Yates Amendment fight, from farmers who raise and store grain on their farms, and from operators of elevators.

In order to clarify the record, I point out that the language of the committee does not anticipate any change in the Department's policy of leaving grain in storage as close to producing areas as possible. . . . I should like to have that type of affirmation and confirmation from the chairman, if he interprets it in the same way.

CHAIRMAN RUSSELL: I had understood from his statement [Senator Monroney's before the subcommittee] that the paragraph related primarily to grain in shipment.[53]

Sometimes the committee refused to allow an interested legislator to use the floor record to modify the committee's report. In the following examples Representatives Reuss (D.-Wisc.) and McGovern (D.-S.D.) wanted to maneuver Representative Anderson (R.-Minn.), ranking member of the Agriculture Subcommittee, into endorsing a stronger wildlife conservation policy. Representatives Reuss and McGovern attempted to establish a floor record that would prohibit any practice with a detrimental effect on waterfowl breeding.

REP. REUSS: Is my understanding correct that the county ACP committees would not be expected to approve practices inconsistent with the observations on p. 18 of the report which I have just read, namely that the Department of Agriculture shall cooperate fully in protecting these lands for wildlife refuges?

REP. McGOVERN: I feel sure the language of the committee report on pages 17 and 18 will provide the kind of intelligent farm drainage without jeopardizing our prairie pothole waterfowl breeding areas.

REP. ANDERSON: . . . the statement in the report is

53. 108 *Congressional Record* 16501 (1962). See also 104 *Congressional Record* 5491 (1958) for a similar example.

in no way to be construed as instructions to any county committee that they can or cannot avail themselves of practices as set forth in the catalog issued by the various state ACP committees. Certainly the language does ask the Department to cooperate *in every way possible*."[54]

Floor debate is employed frequently to reinforce appropriations report directives. Statements made during the floor consideration provide an opportunity for members to stress the importance and benefits of nonstatutory language that affects their districts. Most members know that the amount of legislative history has a cumulative impact that makes it more likely for the administrator to comply. The most direct reinforcement is illustrated by Senator Morse: "I should like the chairman to help me make a legislative record on this subject, because although I am fully aware of what the $400,000 will be used for [since it was elaborated in the report] I believe the record ought to be clear for legislative reference purpose as to what is involved."[55]

Another method consists of threatening an amendment that will transform nonstatutory language into statutory but then withdrawing it after lengthy assurances by the chairman that the appropriations committee feels the report recommendation is mandatory. Representative Bass (D.-Tenn.) started to call up an amendment forbidding construction of a power line to serve the Dixon-Yates combine but then relented because: ". . . I am informed by members of long experience here in the House . . . that the committee report specifically takes care of that; therefore I did not offer the amendment. Therefore, I want the position of this body made absolutely clear."[56]

An effective way to elicit staunch appropriations committee support is to point out that a department has not co-operated in the past, and hence the appropriations committee

---

54. 105 *Congressional Record* 8316 (1959). Emphasis added.
55. 101 *Congressional Record* 7622 (1955), for another example see 107 *Congressional Record* 20989 (1961).
56. 101 *Congressional Record* 8504 (1955).

cannot enforce its report language. In 1958 Senator Young complained that the Agriculture Department ignored a report request to classify some of the cost of price support programs under foreign aid. Accordingly, when the House committee repeated the same request in a subsequent report, Senator Young asked Chairman Russell, "Does the Chairman feel that the Department of Agriculture will come forward with a different budget next year, which will more accurately reflect the cost of price support and other programs." Naturally, Senator Russell responded, the department had better act next year or else suffer stiff consequences.[57]

The most common technique to insure that a nonstatutory device is obligatory involves a compliment of the Appropriations Subcommittee for its fine bill. There is always special praise for the subcommittee's wisdom in approving an item in a particular congressman's district.[58] A colloquy of this type elicits only a simple "thank you" from the subcommittee chairman but does reaffirm Congressional support for the request. Often the chairman will add that he agrees a certain local project is extremely worthwhile.[59]

Occasionally, the floor debate is employed to initiate nonstatutory controls that have not been considered in a prior legislative stage. In fact, entire programs are started or terminated solely on the basis of such discussions on the floor of Congress.

> REP. JENSEN [Chairman of Interior Subcommittee]: Now, there is another thing that is going on that we *direct* the Secretary to prohibit. That is the operation and maintenance by Southwest Power Administration of transmission and other facilities other than those for which Congress has appropriated funds direct to Southwest Power Administration.
> While there is no reference in the bill or the reports

57. 104 *Congressional Record* 6805 (1958).
58. See 101 *Congressional Record* 5730 (1955) concerning fund management in Nevada.
59. See, for instance, 106 *Congressional Record* 10968-80 (1960) where this technique is employed several times.

on this matter [or in the hearings], I want to make it
clear for the record that none of the funds appropriated
by this bill . . . are to be used for the operations and
maintenance by the Southwest Power Administration
of any generation, transmission, or distribution facilities . . . either private or public.[60]

Appropriations committee members, however, sometimes
object to administrators implementing the intent of such
floor colloquies. One such objection was revealed by Chairman Whitten of the House Agriculture Subcommittee:

I have been in Congress twenty-one years. The
explanation given on the floor is seldom if ever complete. It is the last place in the world I would look to
determine fully what Congress meant. What they say
on the floor is to meet an immediate criticism.
I point out that a spelled-out definition means
something, but when you get a fellow in a debate
and they are bearing down on him, he is meeting the
problem of the moment. . . . That is the poorest place
to look for what an act fully means that I know of, to
look to the debate, when the provision is under attack
and the defender is defending his action.[61]

THE CONFERENCE REPORT AND NONSTATUTORY CONTROLS

The final, formal action of the appropriations committee is
embodied in the conference report. Nonstatutory directives
in the statement accompanying conference reports are ordinarily agreed upon by both the House and Senate subcommittees and hence are considered binding.

SEN. HAYDEN: I am not talking about taking chances
in the executive department; I am speaking of the fact
that the Senate must come to an agreement with the
House as to how the $300,000 is to be expended. If in
the conference report it is indicated that the hatchery

60. 99 *Congressional Record* 9997 (1953). Emphasis added.
61. House Hearings on Agriculture Appropriations for 1964, Part 4
(86-1), p. 28.

in Texas is to be built, then the matter certainly is doubly riveted.[62]

There is an important exception, however, to the maxim that mandate language in a conference report is obligatory. By custom only the managers of the House write a statement to accompany a conference report (although both branches sign the report). Hence, the managers of the House are able to insert new nonstatutory instructions or reinforce directives initiated in earlier stages, *without* the assent of the Senate managers.[63] But nonstatutory controls are considered by the Congressional and executive branches as obligatory only when the conference report specifically states that both Houses concur.[64] When the House and Senate managers agree on a directive, the conference report will state "the managers of both Houses agree" rather than "the managers on behalf of the House direct."

REP. JACKSON: I wish to ask the distinguished chairman of the [Senate Interior] subcommittee whether the Senate is bound by the unilateral statement of the House conference in attempting to terminate the [transmission] lines at Goldbar.

REP. CORDON: As the Senator from Washington has so clearly said, the statement on the part of the Managers of the House represents the view of the House conference, not a bilateral statement of the conference. . . . [He goes on to state that the administration is free to build at least one line at Goldbar and concludes:]

. . . The statements on the part of the managers of the House represent the view of the House conference

62. 100 *Congressional Record* 7695 (1954). Emphasis added.
63. See, for instance, 103 *Congressional Record* 10557 (1957).
64. Interviews with members of both branches support this view. However, officials of the National Institutes of Health claim they see no difference if just the House signs the conference report. The House Labor–Health, Education and Welfare Subcommittee feels it has pre-eminence compared to the Senate in the appropriations field, and in addition is more conservative than the Senate committee. This means the House is likely to retaliate if NIH refuses to heed a conference report statement because the Senate managers do not concur.

*in every instance except* where it indicates that the statement is concurred in by the conference of both Houses.[65]

Some Senators object strongly to the fact that House conferees have the last word in conference reports. "As a former member of the House, one of the shocking experiences I had as a new member of the Senate was in discovering that no statement was filed by the Senate conference on a conference report. I think it would be a constructive change if statements in the conference could be signed not only by managers on the part of the House, but also by managers on the part of the Senate."[66]

The conferees are faced with several alternatives with respect to disagreements over report language. Sometimes they are unable to reach an agreement. In such instances, the conference report simply says nothing about the conflict. Indeed, a key difference between statutory and nonstatutory controls is that many nonstatutory disputes are left stalemated by the conferees. For instance, the 1963 House Public Works report states:

> It has come to the Committee's attention that the Area Redevelopment Agency has advanced funds to the Corps of Engineers for the purpose of accomplishing advanced planning and design on a water resources project which is currently pending before the Public Works legislative committee for authorization. . . . The Committee has for some time had an arrangement . . . that advance of funds for . . . moving projects into the planning or construction stages will not be accepted from local interests without the approval of the Committee . . . this arrangement is to preclude the Congress from seeming to be committed to the continuation of a project before having an opportunity to review its merits. . . . The Committee *directs* that the Corps of Engineers and the Bureau of Reclamation hereafter

65. 99 *Congressional Record* 9938 (1953). Emphasis added.
66. 101 *Congressional Record* 7619 (1955).

submit to the committee for prior approval any ARA project.[67]

The Senate report agrees with the House philosophy but claims the ARA situation is an exception. "With respect to this case where work was performed on a reimbursable basis we are faced with a different situation. . . . Under these circumstances the Senate committee would not want to assume operating responsibility to the extent of approving transfers between agencies for work to be performed on a reimbursable basis."[68] There is no statement in the conference report concerning this matter even though the House report contained "mandate language."

An agency response to this type of situation is revealed by a 1958 State Department hearings exchange.

> MR. HALL [Assistant Secretary of State]: . . . that in this point there was some disagreement between the House and Senate reports, and that the final conclusion of the conference report [which was silent on this matter] was, as the Department read the report, that the determination of what the increase would be spent for was left with the Department. . . . It was determined by the Department that certain other projects [than the House earmarked African consular posts] would have a higher priority. . . .[69]

An indication of the importance of nonstatutory controls is that compromises between House and Senate versions of report language are hammered out in the conference. In fact, Senate language is sometimes deliberately phrased so that a larger bargaining area is left for the conference.

> SEN. MUNDT: We felt it would be an unfortunate precedent to establish and that it would be an invasion of States rights to have that kind of mandatory language in the report. It is my hope that by highlighting

67. House Report (87-2223), p. 3. Emphasis added.
68. Senate Report (87-2178), p. 27.
69. House Hearings on State Department Appropriations for 1959 (85-2), pp. 33-34.

this matter [through offsetting language in the Senate report] we can sit across the table during the conference, and that the conference report may contain language which will adjust the points of view and make it clear that neither the mandatory provisions of the House report or the Senate report represent the opinion of the Congress, and find some way to iron out the matter in the conference report.[70]

A well-publicized case involving a compromise between the two Houses resolved the 1961 controversy concerning the Upper Colorado River Transmission Division. From the outset it was evident that the private utilities would use every means to prevent construction of government transmission lines for preference customers (who by federal law are entitled to priority in purchasing power from Federal projects). Chairman Clarence Cannon characterized the legislative activity surrounding the House Appropriations Committee as follows: "The power trust is making the most carefully organized and most determined fight against these transmission lines that I have ever seen since I have been in the House. They are concentrating on the members of the subcommittees by mail and telegram and telephone and will be able to intimidate many members of Congress."[71]

Nevertheless, the House Appropriations Committee submitted its report recommending, without any conditions, appropriation of the full amount requested by the secretary of the Interior to construct the all-federal system. So hot was the House legislative fight that President Kennedy aided in the passage of the House bill."[72]

Undaunted, the private companies continued their efforts with the Senate Public Works Subcommittee and met with some success. The Senate recommended appropriation of the full presidential request, but the report implied the most controversial lines should be *replaced by wheeling agree-*

70. 101 *Congressional Record* 7619 (1955).
71. See House Hearings on Public Works Appropriations for 1963 (87-2), pp. 23-28.
72. *Ibid.*, pp. 25-26.

*ments* with private utilities.[73] The conference report compromised the nonstatutory language by stating that the government power lines should be started only if the Secretary could not reach wheeling agreements with public utilities that were in the national interest. "The conferees on the part of both Houses are in agreement that the planning and construction of transmission lines for the Colorado River storage project shall proceed as provided for in the budget . . . unless the Secretary finds it practicable and in the national interest to enter into wheeling agreements with private power interests."[74]

Compromises of report language are relatively infrequent when compared to conference compromises on nonstatutory money earmarks. If the two Houses disagree on the amount of a nonstatutory budget decrease, the conference report will usually contain the mutually acceptable figure.[75]

The conferees may agree that the administration should disregard House report comments in favor of the Senate version (or vice-versa). In 1953 the House Interior report imposed several restrictions on the administration of saline water research grants.[76] The Senate report countered with the view that the administrator should be allowed the "broadest discretion in disbursing the research money."[77] The conference report stated, "The conferees endorse the language in the Senate report with regard to this appropriation item."[78]

The conference report furnishes the initial opportunity for the House to reinforce nonstatutory controls initiated in the Senate report. Also, the House conferees are sometimes able to persuade their Senate colleagues that certain directives are worthy of stress by both Houses. In 1960 the House Labor–Health, Education and Welfare report stated that the com-

73. *Ibid.*, pp. 25-26. Emphasis is added.
74. *Ibid.*, p. 27.
75. House Report (87-1268), p. 24. Emphasis added. For a more lengthy example, see House Report (85-1776), p. 4.
76. House Report (83-314), p. 3.
77. Senate Report (83-613), p. 8.
78. 99 *Congressional Record* 9990 (1953). For another example see House Report (83-947) with regard to the Missouri diversion unit.

mittee "expected" additional amounts would be spent on milk, shellfish, and general inspection, even though the committee had not altered the budget request. Evidently the conferees learned that the Environmental Health Division was going to disregard the House if the Senate did not concur. Therefore, the conference report stated the Congressional intent more forcefully. "It is obvious that the Department has failed to carry out the desires of the House. . . . The *conferees are agreed* that the Department should consider the House report on this matter as being instructions."[79] Note the substitution of mandate language "instructs" for "expects."[80]

Some nonstatutory controls are initiated in conference reports without consideration in prior stages of the appropriations process.[81] In 1953 the Interior Conference Committee directed the Southwest Power Administration to cancel contracts with five Rural Electrification Administration generation and transmission co-operatives. The contracts enable the Southwest Power Administration to lease and operate REA transmission systems. Opponents of the following directive claimed it would cripple REA power co-operatives for the benefit of private power combines. "None of the funds allowed [to Southwest Power Administration] are to be used for the purpose of implementing existing contracts with lease purchases of transmission or generating facilities. The funds may be used only for . . . payment of wheeling service charges at rates and in amounts comparable to those paid in the Southwest Power Administration area under existing contracts."[82]

In 1957 the House committee decided to "direct" the disposal of an oil shale plant in the conference report despite strong Senate objections. Neither the House nor Senate said anything about disposing of the Rifle, Colorado, plant in 1957 prior to the conference report. This meant that the

79. 105 *Congressional Record* 14744 (1959). Conference report is reprinted in *Congressional Record*.
80. 105 *Congressional Record* 14744 (1959). Emphasis added. Conference report is reprinted in *Congressional Record*.
81. 101 *Congressional Record* 9069 (1955). Emphasis added.
82. 99 *Congressional Record* 9995 (1953).

floor debate on the conference bill—the final stage of the appropriations process—was of crucial importance for Senators who wanted to establish an offsetting legislative record.

SEN. ALLOT [R.-Colo.]: I emphasize the statement that the managers on part of the House direct that all buildings shall be disposed of. I should like to ask whether the managers on the part of the Senate agreed to any such provision.

SEN. HAYDEN [Chairman]: We did not. I want to make it clear that the statement referred to is the statement of the managers on the part of the House and in no way reflects the views of the Senate conferees.

It is my personal view, which I think is shared by all the Senate conferees, that the disposition of these facilities was not a matter before the conference committee (since neither report specified disposition). The only question before the conference committee was the amount to be appropriated for maintenance and protection of these facilities.

I understand that there is pending proposed legislation dealing with the future use of this installation. Therefore, it is a matter for the appropriate legislative committee and the Congress.

SEN. ALLOT: . . . what is the legislative effect of the direction?

SEN. HAYDEN: It may be persuasive upon those interested in the matter either to do something *or do nothing.* Anyway, the two Houses have not agreed. The recommendation made does not carry the force of the law *or the force of a united conference report.*[83]

Professor Fenno has demonstrated that the floor debate on the conference report is usually anticlimatic, and consumes, on the average, about 3.2 pages in the *Record* or 30 minutes.[84] Consequently, this stage of the appropriations process is the least important with respect to statutory or nonstatutory controls.

83. 103 *Congressional Record* 10610 (1957). Emphasis added.
84. See Richard Fenno, *The Power of the Purse: Appropriations Politics in Congress* (Boston: Little, Brown and Co., 1966), pp. 672-73.

## Government without Passing Laws

While the statute can be amended solely during the formal stages of the appropriations process, nonstatutory controls are altered through informal communications between administrators and legislators. After the bill is passed, it is standard procedure for administrators to "appeal" what they believe to be unreasonable or unwise nonstatutory recommendations. On occasion, executive officials are successful in obtaining subcommittee acquiescence to proposed changes. The interim meetings throughout the year, which Professor MacMahon analyzed in 1943, are partly concerned with off the record adjustments of report language.[85]

Interview data reveals that the Corps of Engineers "appeals" the largest number of nonstatutory directives. This is simply because the bulk of corps construction activities are regulated by nonstatutory devices. The act includes a lump sum for the construction of many projects, but the allocation for each separate project is in the report. The report is filled, moreover, with subcommittee recommendations as to the specifications and procedure that should be used in construction. Corps personnel, when referring to directives they feel are unreasonable or ill-advised, remarked "these things are negotiable."

> We can back them [the subcommittees] down with technical information showing the unfortunate effects of obeying their instructions. They can rationalize they did not have the information as an excuse for letting us off the hook. To change a nonstatutory directive we call the staff man who if he thinks our case is justified, asks us to send some supporting technical information. He discusses it with the chairman and ranking member and if they agree, they phone or write us and 'amend' the nonstatutory directive—or even say forget it.

85. See Arthur W. MacMahon, "Congressional Oversight of Administration: The Power of the Purse," *Political Science Quarterly*, 58 (1943), pp. 161-90.

The Corps contacts both House and Senate subcommittees, not just the subcommittee that originated the extralegal language. The relationship between the corps and the subcommittee's staff was so cordial that the staff man, if he was not swayed, would suggest that the Corps take its case directly to the chairman. The chairman and the ranking minority member make virtually all decisions on these appeals and rarely consult with the rest of the subcommittee.

A similar procedure is followed by other agencies and departments but with some notable variations. Like most nonstatutory procedures, the procedures for informal adjustments depend to a great extent on custom and personalities. For instance, when Agriculture Department administrators appeal nonstatutory directives, they go directly to the chairman and never contact the staff first. National Institute of Health officials are very reluctant to appeal over the head of the staff to the subcommittee. As one Health, Education and Welfare administrator put it: "The staff man can do you a lot of favors, and if you antagonize him it can really hurt you later on."

If the nonstatutory directive is important enough, *ad hoc* sessions of the entire Labor–Health, Education and Welfare Subcommittee are convened to meet with departmental officers.[86] Regardless of which procedure is followed, a State Department budget officer stressed that it is often difficult to win appeals on nonstatutory instructions because "it looks bad for the committee to back down on something it justifies before the whole House.[87]

Occasionally, evidence of such "post-passage negotiations" appears in the printed record. In 1954 the Southwest Power Administration wanted to extend its contracts with the Rural Electrification Administration co-operatives past the July

86. The Corps of Engineers have also had interim meetings with the subcommittee.

87. As we have seen, some appropriation committee members expressed the view that the whole House approves the entire report at the same time they approve the bill.

deadline specified in the 1953 conference report. During the House hearings SWPA officials asked subcommittee Chairman Jensen how this might be done. He replied: "Matters of that nature are generally handled by a letter from the Senate and House committees approving such a procedure. . . . We would like to have a letter from Interior setting out the situation on which the subcommittee will take action pro or con. I would suggest you also send the Senate committee a similar letter."[88]

A successful departmental appeal is demonstrated by the efforts of the Department of Agriculture to reduce detailed reporting requirements for overseas competitive sales of surplus commodities.

> REP. WHITTEN [Chairman]: . . . Some years ago this committee insisted that the Secretary report monthly . . . concerning sales for dollars. Subsequent to that I have had several requests that we forego any such request. . . . As far as I am concerned, if you keep us advised, with perhaps less detail, but in letter form, the month to month situation, it might serve the same purpose. In other words, if you want to scale it down.[89]

Usually the subcommittee decision on an executive appeal is communicated through informal off-the-record channels. However, at times the committee wants to detail the change in its report. During 1961 the Corps of Engineers objected to a stipulation that local interests must contribute 20 per cent to local projects.[90] The 1962 report stated: "Testimony . . . indicates that this would impose an undue hardship on certain projects where local interests have made previous contributions by initially constructing their own protective works. In view of this the committee intends to modify its position to the extent of permitting such prior

88. House Hearings on Interior Appropriations for 1955 (83-2), p. 103.
89. House Hearings on Agriculture Department Appropriations for 1963 (87-2), pp. 1990-91.
90. This information was disclosed during interviews.

investments to be included in calculating the 20% contribution."[91]

There is not enough public record to judge the frequency and importance of "post-passage negotiations." It is clear that the chairman and the ranking minority member play the key role in this process. The other members of the subcommittee are rarely consulted.

SUMMARY AND CONCLUSION

The complexity of the numerous relationships and interactions is the striking thing about this analysis of nonstatutory controls as they pass through the stages of the appropriations process. Some nonstatutory controls involve only one stage—a Senate report for instance—and can be explained without becoming entangled in conference report action, Senate endorsement, "mandate language," and the like. On the other hand, a number of policy-laden directives are modified in almost every stage—and even in "post-passage negotiations."

By contrast, statutory control is *relatively* uncomplicated and precise. The final compromise between the House and the Senate is set forth in the act, and in theory all language in the statute is uniformly binding. Generally, language in the act is more carefully thought out and worded. Granting the ambiguity and differences of interpretation involved in any law, statutory control appears straightforward when compared to nonstatutory devices.

Only administrators aware of the fine points and customs surrounding nonstatutory techniques can perceive the difference among Congressional doubts, advice, suggestions, and mandates. Usually, discovering this difference depends on analyzing and harmonizing Congressional action in several legislative stages. This entire process is complicated by bicameralism, since the two Houses may conflict and never clearly point out their final agreement—or even reach an agreement.

From the administrator's point of view, several factors

91. House Report (87-2223), p. 40.

affect the degree to which any particular directive is regarded as obligatory. Is "mandate language" used? Is the point raised in hearings, and, if so, is it dwelt upon? If the Senate report is silent, does this indicate that the Senate subcommittee is opposed? Does the whole House give unusual attention to the item in question? Is the language in the conference report endorsed by the managers of both Houses?

Similarly, from a Congressional viewpoint considerable ambiguity surrounds this method of oversight. Members who are not on the appropriations committees do not comprehend which circumstances make report langauge mandatory or permissive. This attitude is evidenced by frequent requests for the subcommittee chairman to explain whether nonstatutory language is binding.[92]

Indeed, in some situations veteran appropriations committee members cannot agree on what nonstatutory control implies. The 1954 House Interior Report stated that the House committee had information that a public utility may be willing to construct transmission lines to connect the Davis Dam distribution system. The report continues, "Should the utility which owns this plant make an acceptable proposition, the committee *instructs* the Secretary to accept their proposal."[93] The secretary ignored the House report because the conference report included the amount for the government transmission line with no additional comment. Since the public utilities subsequently made a proposal, Representatives Budge and Jensen could not agree as to whether the Bureau of Reclamation improperly disregarded Congressional intent.

> REP. BUDGE [R.-Idaho]: I am quite surprised to find that, I believe, $111,000 was spent last fiscal year, in

92. Already covered in the preceding section are the Upper Colorado River transmission dispute, competitive sales of agriculture commodities, SWPA (Southwest Power Administration) and REA (Rural Electrification Administration) co-operative contracts, new health programs for retarded children, and the Dixon-Yates and Trinity River projects.

93. House Hearings on Interior Appropriations for 1955 (83-2), p. 941. Emphasis added.

spite of the House language. It seems to me there could have been checking back with the committee to get around the language that the committee intentionally put in the committee report.

REP. JENSEN [Chairman]: I guess the only answer to that, Mr. Budge, is that we did not insert any language in the conference report, which is the final action of the committees of Congress. In this respect, as in all others, if we failed to get instructions in the conference report, then it is assumed by the Bureau, since there was no mention of it in the conference report where the House committee also sits, that the House committee has agreed that this item could be included in the final bill.

REP. BUDGE: That might present a very interesting legislative interpretation. I am not sure of the fact that [if] the conference committee is silent upon the prohibition which has been placed in the House report, [it] doesn't mean just the reverse, the conferees concur in the previous [House] report. Just mere silence in there [a conference report] doesn't seem to me to, as you say, countermand the language in the House report.

REP. JENSEN: You may be right, but I think you will find that the Bureau of Reclamation, as do all other agencies of the government, takes the conference report as the final consensus of the Congress.[94]

94. House Hearings on Interior Appropriations for 1955 (83-2), p. 941. The writer's opinion is that in a case of this type, conference report silence does not countermand the House report but rather diminishes its binding force (assuming the Senate report made no comment on the House directive).

# III. *Enforcing Nonstatutory Controls*

Since most senior members of any appropriations subcommittee are from "safe districts," the relationship between subcommittee and agency officials is a continuing one. Administrators stress the importance of a "good working relationship" with subcommittee members who handle the annual agency appropriations.[1] One means to attain this relationship is to implement the subcommittee's nonstatutory recommendations. On the other hand, a sure way to create Congressional antipathy and restrictions is to frequently disregard report language.

Since administrators prefer the flexibility inherent in nonstatutory controls, a subcommittee will employ fewer statutory restrictions when it can trust the agency to follow legislative intent. Other frequent benefits of "a good working relationship" are increased appropriations, greater ability to transfer funds, and some additional freedom from central executive controls.

Professor Fenno has stressed that agency perceptions of the appropriations committee are dominated by a sense of uncertainty. A major agency goal is a stable relationship with the committee to permit orderly program planning and operation. One obvious way to minimize uncertainty is to follow nonstatutory guidance given by the committee.[2]

This does not mean, however, that the appropriations subcommittees never encounter enforcement problems. Even though statutory controls are self-enforcing as the law of the land, the General Accounting Office and the Treasury check on

1. Aaron B. Wildavsky, *Politics of the Budgetary Process* (Boston: Little, Brown and Co., 1964), p. 74.
2. See Richard Fenno, *The Power of the Purse: Appropriations Politics in Congress* (Boston: Little, Brown and Co., 1966), pp. 291-93.

administrative compliance[3] As a consequence, subcommittees do not concern themselves to any great extent with enforcement of statutory language.[4] On the other hand, since non-statutory controls are not legally binding, the subcommittees must employ their own resources to enforce them.

The annual hearings provide the principal forum for subcommittees to monitor nonstatutory controls. Administrators expect a follow-through, because the subcommittees are repetitive; they repeat the same questions and pursue the same objectives. An Agriculture Department official stated that he had no idea what the provisos are in the law, but he can recite the report comments that Chairman Whitten feels are important. A typical committee inquiry follows:

> Rep. Cannon [Chairman]: Last year we asked you [in the report] to reinstate, reactivate certain contracts. To what extent have you [Corps of Engineers] been able to comply?[5]

An example of a committee compliment is included in the fiscal 1957 State Department Appropriation: "The committee was again pleased to learn that foreign grantees [of the International Education Exchange] are being placed wherever possible in the smaller colleges . . . as originally proposed by this committee and urges the Department to strengthen this trend."[6]

The Corps of Engineers, like many agencies, is so accustomed to inquiries that it volunteers the information in the opening statement at the annual appropriations hearing.

> Major General Stringer [Chief Engineer for Civil Works]: The Appropriation Committees in their re-

3. Lucius Wilmerding, Jr., *Spending Power* (New Haven: Yale University Press, 1943), *passim*, proves that statutory controls are ineffective in some cases, but the writer believes such cases are not nearly as numerous as Wilmerding implies.

4. Much time is spent in the hearings checking on compliance with nonstatutory directions, virtually none for statutory restrictions.

5. House Hearings on Public Works Appropriations for 1956 (84-2), p. 108.

6. Senate Report (84-2034), p. 6.

ports last year indicated an interest in certain problems and requested specific action in some cases. I would like to discuss briefly our action on a number of the most important points raised.[7]

An agency's working relationship, built up over several years with an appropriations subcommittee, will not be jeopardized without a careful consideration as to the consequences. The success of the committee's enforcement efforts is illustrated by the following incident. The "order" Mr. Wright refers to is a report directive.

> MR. WRIGHT [Director, Southwest Power Administration]: I have learned to obey orders from the Congressmen, and when I am given an order [after having] submitted my recommendations, if they are contrary to it, I try to obey the order.[8]

However, this apparently docile and submissive attitude can vanish when an administrator concludes that nonstatutory language will prevent implementation of crucial policy. Again a statement by Mr. Wright: "This direction is contained in a committee report of what the intent of Congress is as to the implementation of these contracts. I think it is a rather general direction. I do not think it specifically changes the status of the flood control act, which vests certain responsibilities and authorities on the Secretary [of the Interior], and which I do not believe can be changed by a committee report."[9]

The limits of nonstatutory controls are highlighted by this exchange between former Deputy Under-Secretary of State Henderson and Chairman Rooney (D.-N.Y.) of the State Department Appropriations Subcommittee.

7. House Hearings on Public Works Appropriations for 1956 (84-2), p. 61. A request for a progress report is a useful tool for securing compliance and helps overcome the inherent weaknesses of nonstatutory control. See Senate Report (87-1578), p. 44.

8. *Ibid.*, p. 140. As the following paragraph indicates, this administrator is not as servile as the quotation implies.

9. Senate Hearings on Public Works Appropriations for 1957 (84-2), p. 396.

CHAIRMAN ROONEY: This is probably just a waste of time, but it is the usual thing with the Department of State year after year. Here in connection with 1957 program you cut out new posts which you insisted you had to have [and consequently the committee earmarked them in the report] and then you fatten ones which you had open.

MR. HENDERSON: I would like to point out that we do take into consideration—very serious consideration—the recommendations made by this committee, and I think you will find we have carried out *most* of them. Sometimes, however, in our operations we are up against difficulties and we feel this committee would like for us to have a certain amount of *discretion* when we do find difficult situations facing us. If we have exceeded our discretion, I greatly regret it, but I would like to make clear that we do respect the views of this committee, and we do try to carry them out. Only when we think *it is in the national interest* . . . do we take any action which is not strictly in accordance with the recommendations of this committee.

REP. ROONEY: When you feel like it, you just disregard everything the committee says. That would be a fair conclusion from what you say. You know more about the national interest.

MR. HALL [Deputy Under-Secretary of State]: There are times when we have to make a choice, when the funds available do not permit us to do what we would like to do on both sides of the Capitol, and I think we have given those decisions . . . every consideration. We do respect the committee and try to follow the committee reports.

REP. ROONEY: These self-serving declarations, Mr. Secretary, do not mean a thing. The committee is not running the Executive Branch of the Government.[10]

Bold administrators who refuse to observe the committee's nonstatutory instructions are not exceptional. In a classic statement after World War II, General Clay refused to fol-

10. House Hearings on State Department Appropriations for 1959 (85-2), pp. 33-34. Emphasis added.

low a House report directive concerning de-Nazification because he "would rather forego financial support than sacrifice our objectives."[11] Many executives have refused to be bound by earmarked amounts, based on budget estimates one and a half years old.[12] At times noncompliance is not grounded in any high motive, however, but reflects bureaucratic inertia and inability to implement economies rapidly.

There are numerous examples in the printed record of the limits of nonstatutory controls.[13] It is not surprising to find that the use of hearings as an *independent technique* often proves to be ineffective.

> REP. ROONEY: In how many years, Mr. Secretary, has the House Appropriations Committee been talking about getting you to do something about reducing the cost of these transfers? . . . At least in your recollection 3 or 4 years. . . . And still you are "analyzing" and still permit a situation to exist where these two firms have the inside track on getting your employees to use their services.[14]

Although recommendations made in the reports are considered more binding, the administrator sometimes disregards language that has been reiterated in several reports of both Houses.

> Despite the committee of Congress repeatedly insisting [in its report] that the Bureau [of Reclamation] carry out the originally contemplated procedure with reference to the operation and maintenance of irrigation projects by local interests, little, if any effective action has been taken. The committee is at a loss to understand this reluctance on the part of the Bureau. In the absence of more positive action on the

11. Holbert N. Carroll, *House of Representatives and Foreign Affairs* (Pittsburgh: University of Pittsburgh Press, 1958), p. 165.

12. See Senate Hearings on State Department Appropriations for 1955 (83-2), p. 1135.

13. The following cases involve unambiguous nonstatutory directives that could not be ignored on the basis of confusion over intent.

14. House Hearings on State Department Appropriations for 1960 (96-1), p. 54.

part of the Bureau, it can only be assumed that such inactivity in this regard results . . . from a desire of the Bureau to perpetuate itself as a Federal bureaucracy. . . .[15]

Another example of the limits of report language: "Although the committee has repeatedly expressed concern over the costs of our membership in these international organizations, this appropriation has nearly doubled in the last five years. Testimony presented by Department of State witnesses does not reflect sufficient efforts being exerted to hold the annual budgets of these organizations to a minimum."[16]

No matter what steps a subcommittee takes to make report language binding, administrators will not comply in some situations. There are several cases in which administrators have ignored strongly worded report directives that are reinforced by floor speeches.[17] Techniques designed to make a directive obligatory, however, are crucial in situations where the administrator is reluctant, but not determined, to disregard the appropriations committee.

It seems easier for the appropriations committee to enforce negative prohibitions than to secure satisfactory enforcement of affirmative directives.[18] Nonstatutory techniques are usually most effective when they disallow money for an activity or direct discontinuance of administrative procedures. However, if the committee report prescribes a definite course of action designed to improve efficiency, it is ordinarily complied with.

Nonstatutory directives that call for increased efficiency without making any specific proposals, or for greater diligence in administering certain parts of an act, meet with less success. In 1962, the House report stated with regard to Atomic En-

15. Senate Hearings on Public Works Appropriations for 1957 (84-2), p. 357. House report is reprinted in the Senate hearings.

16. House Report (87-1996), p. 6.

17. See, for instance, 101 *Congressional Record* 3848 (1955) regarding FHA loans for housing and farm ownership.

18. See Elias Huzar, "Legislative Control over Administration: Congress and the W.P.A.," *American Political Science Review*, 36 (1942), 257ff, for an identical conclusion.

ergy Commission physical research: "The committee is convinced that the funds made available in this program are not producing returns commensurate with the investment, and insists that there be tighter controls on research grants to assure that they are being effectively used."[19]

This directive is of a positive nature, and typical of the type of nonstatutory language that is difficult to enforce. Often the agency buries the substance of the directive in a face-saving communication to the effect that the agency is trying hard to improve performance.[20]

The underlying reason for inadequate response to some positive directives appears to be bureaucratic inertia and resistance to change. Even though the committee remains dissatisfied, it lacks the knowledge to specify in a proviso what efficiency measures need to be initiated. In the above case, only the administrator dealing with the individual Atomic Energy Commission research applications can make this judgment on a case-by-case basis. Similarly, the appropriations committee does not have the *expertise* to initiate a broad-scale attack on big city problems if the executive refuses to heed report prodding.

Often, nonstatutory controls cannot prevent the transfer of funds among the detailed estimates presented at the appropriations hearings. Neither the law nor the report specifies fund allocations in nearly as great detail as the estimates, justification, and remarks administrators make in the hearings. But the estimates are so detailed that to expect complete adherence would be unrealistic.

The executive's problem is to distinguish allowable from improper types of deviation.[21] On numerous occasions the detailed estimates are ignored to such an extent that the appropriations committee feels it is justified in protesting. On the other hand, the executive believes it must not be bound by

19. House Report (87-2223), p. 61.
20. Carroll, *House of Representatives and Foreign Affairs*, p. 165.
21. See Arthur W. MacMahon, "Congressional Oversight of the Administration: The Power of the Purse," *Political Science Quarterly*, 58 (1943), 402.

a detailed budget based on forecasts for a year and a half in advance. The appropriations committees reply that the American governmental system stands for control of the purse by elected representatives not arbitrary executives.

MR. STEIBERT [Director, USIA]: Now they may be well suited, the amount you are using for each, for a particular objective in a country today. It may change, in that country in 6 months, and you may want to establish some other kind of program. . . . Or you are under the necessity now of forecasting . . . a year and a half in advance, the total amount which you will need to spend in various countries or in various areas. All of which is an attempt to show that a coordinated effort and flexibility among media are required to produce the best results for the money spent.

SEN. KNOWLAND [R.-Calif.]: I think you have to keep in mind the Congressional reaction to a situation where they [an agency] would come up and justify a military installation and make such an overwhelming case that the committee would unanimously approve it . . . and if next year we came back and found that having gotten the money out of us . . . they had used the money on something else . . . it takes the control of the pursestrings away from Congress and you can do that to where you are making one blanket appropriation with entire discretion in the hands of the executive.

Now, as I say, a very desirable case could be made on that from the executive viewpoint, but Government is a little different from business and long ago the people who had some experience with arbitrary monarchies decided they were going to replace control of the public purse in the hands of elected representatives. . . . Congress is going to insist on maintaining control of the funds and when justifications are made to it and they are based on those justifications, appropriate the funds . . . they are going to be insulted if there is a major change in policy.[22]

22. Senate Hearings on State Department Appropriations for 1955 (83-2), p. 1135.

In fact, the appropriations committees are unable to prevent the departments from transferring funds contrary to non-statutory earmarks in the report.[23] Moreover, agency accounting systems and budget presentations frequently make it difficult for Congress to ascertain whether funds are spent in accordance with the specific report earmarks. Statutory limitations require a separate account that is reviewed by the General Accounting Office. A separate account is rarely instituted for amounts earmarked in committee reports.

An enforcement problem also results from the limited effective time span of nonstatutory controls. Indeed, there is some disagreement among subcommittees as to what extent a change in committee leadership alters the force of previous report language. Chairman Buseby (R.-Ill.) of the Labor–Health, Education and Welfare Subcommittee indicated in 1954 that: "One committee cannot bind another committee. This committee can decide to take the wishes of the Public Health Service in this matter or it can reaffirm the position the committee took when the gentleman from Wisconsin, Mr. Steele, was Chairman."[24]

After the initial year, Congressional staff concurs that the enforcement of nonstatutory language is on a random basis and rarely thorough.[25] Their attitude stems from the annual basis of appropriation bills, which appears to support the view that nonstatutory directives apply only to a single year's funds. There are, however, important exceptions to this general rule. Indeed, report instructions that are important to the chairman or to any other member may be enforced five years later. The vast amount of nonstatutory controls in each appropriations cycle, however, makes it impossible for one or two subcom-

23. See, for instance, House Report (83-1510), p. 3. The proper method for transferring funds from a Congressional viewpoint will be considered in a subsequent chapter.

24. House Hearings on Labor–Health, Education and Welfare Appropriations for 1955 (83-2), p. 153.

25. Army Corps of Engineers employees said the committee was of "one mind" regardless of changes in the party controlling Congress. Consequently, this limited time span does not pertain to reports on Army Corps appropriations.

mittee staff members to check on compliance after the initial year.

Interviews reveal that the executive branch is well aware of this limited enforcement of nonstatutory directives after the first year. Some administrators claim they disregard the ones they find objectionable. On balance, if the committee wants to tie down extralegal language, it must state in subsequent reports that the committee views "are still valid."[26] "The committee recommends continuation in 1961 of the provision in the [1960] conference report . . . providing that funds made available for acquisition of lands in Civil War areas [by the National Park Service] are not to be obligated until the Secretary, has reported to the Committee on Appropriations that local Governments have adopted adequate zoning regulations to assure against future commercial development in these areas."[27]

The limitations described above are the exceptions and not the rule. In fact, disregard of nonstatutory techniques is rare. The interview responses were so uniform and emphatic that it was not necessary to explore the extent of noncompliance through a detailed enumeration of the printed record. In some cases the administrative response is a token gesture, but even this is infrequent in view of the necessity to maintain good relations with the appropriations committee.

The prevalent attitude of administrators with regard to nonstatutory directives is "we just have to live with them." Administrators quickly add, however, that nonstatutory control has its advantages of flexibility and must be observed to insure this flexibility in the future.

THE USE OF SANCTIONS

In most situations the appropriations committees possess sanctions that can overcome the inherent weaknesses of nonstatutory techniques. An appropriations subcommittee that

26. See Senate Report (87-294), p. 6.
27. Senate Hearings on Interior appropriations for 1961 (87-1), p. 1092. House Report is reprinted in the Senate hearings.

determines an agency's money supply possesses a number of potent means to enforce its will. Sanctions used by the appropriations committees can be classified in three groups—sanctions that are not part of the statute, statutory sanctions that affect the administrator's fund level, and statutory sanctions unrelated to specific fund levels.

A severe rebuke in the hearings is usually an adequate deterrent against future nonobservance.[28] Indeed a verbal reprimand can be so violent that, as one Agriculture Department employee declared, "I don't care what happens, I don't want to ever go through something like that again in my life." Chairman Whitten of the House Agriculture Subcommittee had eliminated ten pages of heated exchanges before the record was published.

In 1955 Joseph Kelly, chairman of the Railroad Retirement Board, promised to send the House Labor–Health, Education and Welfare Subcommittee the legal authority under which he could deny Navaho Indians unemployment benefits for six months. The subcommittee never received the requested communication, and the following year Mr. Kelly spent a very painful day on Capitol Hill. Chairman Fogarty berated Kelly for several minutes because of his "contemptuous attitude toward the committee."[29]

Another potent sanction that does not involve the use of the statute is the "punitive investigation." Such an investigation is designed to embarrass and to arouse disapproval of an agency by the public or an influential group.[30] "Punitive investigations" are not usually caused by any isolated incident but rather by a series of administrative actions.

A classic example is the refusal of the Commodity Credit Corporation to follow repeated House and Senate report in-

28. See House Hearings on Labor–Health, Education and Welfare Appropriations for 1957 (84-2), p. 360.
29. For an example of such a statement see House Hearings on Labor–Health, Education and Welfare Appropriations for 1960 (86-1), p. 488. Mr. Kelly agreed to comply with the subcommittee's wishes (p. 489).
30. See Morgan Thomas, "Appropriations Control and the Atomic Energy Program," *Western Political Quarterly*, 9 (1956), 714

structions to sell cotton abroad at competitive prices. When the CCC did not respond, the House subcommittee began to investigate many aspects of CCC operations. These investigations by a special staff were very critical of the CCC's general performance and policies. Over three hundred pages of the 1959 House hearings concerned this multi-ranging investigation.[31]

The most obvious statutory sanction is the power of the purse. A large cut in an agency's budget request cannot only deter future noncompliance but also provides an example for other administrators to see and to shun. "The Committee recommends a reduction of $50,000 under the House allowance and $100,000 under the budget estimate. The Committee is unable to discern any results from its suggestion *in the past several years,* accompanying its new recommendations for increased allowances, that the Bureau [of Public Assistance] make a concerted effort to impress upon the States the need for effecting every economy."[32]

An outstanding example of the power of the purse involved the 1954 U.N. technical assistance program. Both the legislative committee and the administration were highly enthusiastic about this program. The House Appropriations Committee, however, did not recommend any money for technical assistance because the State Department ignored the report. In 1953 the committee stated that it "desired" that all U.N. contributions be placed under one heading in the State Department budget and "believed" that the U.S. contribution should be limited to one-third rather than the customary one-half of the technical assistance program. When the State Department did not respond, Chairman Rooney declared, "I think this might be a good place to see that the language in the House committee report is adhered to by the Department of State." This type of U.N. assistance was never resumed.[33]

The U.N. technical assistance case indicates that the ulti-

31. See House Hearings on Agriculture Appropriations for 1960 (86-1), *passim.*
32. Senate Report (83-478), p. 20. Emphasis added.
33. Carroll, *House of Representatives and Foreign Affairs,* p. 52.

mate sanction of an appropriations cut is caused frequently by an accumulation of past noncompliance rather than one incident. Many subcommittees have cut requests drastically over minor issues or in instances where mandate language has not been employed.[34] Thus, if an agency has disregarded prior directives, it can never tell at what point noncompliance will occasion a substantial cut.

A substantial appropriations cut can be an excessively blunt sanction. For example, in 1957 the House committee decided to take drastic action after report language failed to persuade the Bureau of Reclamation to turn the operation and maintenance of irrigation projections over to local users. "Such lethargy on the part of those responsible . . . leaves the committee with no alternative but to reduce the funds requested for operation and maintenance with the sincere hope that it will force prompt assumption of proper responsibility by local water users and the Bureau in this program."[35] Senator Hayden pointed out that this statutory cut penalized the innocent as well as the guilty. Many uncompleted projects had to be cut back, and local users cannot be expected to assume the operation of uncompleted projects.[36]

The committee has two types of sanctions that do not affect specific fund levels but impose objectionable restrictions. The "punitive proviso" usually constrains administrative flexibility to a greater extent than the nonstatutory directive it is intended to enforce. In 1954 the House Labor–Health, Education and Welfare Subcommittee discovered that the office of the secretary of Health, Education and Welfare was transferring funds to activities the report had deleted. In prior

34. For another example of a cut in funds caused by noncompliance with nonstatutory controls see Morgan Thomas, "Appropriations Control and the Atomic Energy Commission," p. 723. The House report "recommended reductions in Atomic Energy Commission operations management fees in fiscal 1949 and 1950, but the AEC did not reduce the fees. After this unsatisfactory response, the House Appropriations Committee included in the fiscal 1951 bill a dollar limit that cut these fees in half.

35. Senate Hearings on Public Works Appropriations for 1957 (84-2), p. 363, reprint of House report.

36. *Ibid.*, p. 363.

years the Departments of Labor and Health, Education and Welfare had held the authority to transfer up to 5 per cent of the salaries and expenses of any appropriation. As a result of this incident the Senate Appropriations Committee inserted a "punitive proviso" that lowered the HEW transfer authority to 1 per cent. The Labor Department was warned that it maintained the 5 per cent transfer authority only as long as the privilege was not abused.[37]

An excellent example of the "punitive proviso" is included in the 1965 Labor–Health, Education and Welfare bill. The committee inserted an amendment prohibiting the use of funds for any activity in excess of the amount set forth in the detailed schedules of the President's budget.

> The conferees are agreed that this is a very important program, but the managers on the part of *both* the House and Senate do not in any way condone the actions of . . . starting this program before a single dollar has been appropriated for the purpose. . . . Both the Department of Labor and HEW have continued to abuse legal flexibility which they have been allowed by Congress in the face of *continued informal warnings.* And, at times *reprogramming* has at least bordered on the illegal. In view of this, the conferees have taken action in connection with amendment No. 62 which should have a salutory effect.[38]

A second type of legal sanction that does not include a budget reduction involves the number of statutory line items. The trend in recent years has been towards a statutory lump-sum appropriation, in place af detailed specifications of purpose. The administrator can transfer easily within the lump sum to meet contingencies. From a Congressional viewpoint, however, the lump-sum appropriation is not intended to permit transfer of funds in excess of the amount specified in the committee report. When the State Department abused the

37. Senate Report (83-1623), p. 13.
38. House Report (88-1880), p. 7. Emphasis added.

Government without Passing Laws

flexibility of its appropriation for "Salaries and Expenses," the Congress simply appropriated on a detailed line-item basis.[39]

To prevent a committee sanction, executives have a standard procedure that advises that the committee nonstatutory controls will be ignored: "It doesn't pay to try to put something over on them [committee members] because if you get caught you might as well pack your bags and leave Washington."[40]

The initial step is to explain why the agency feels it is unable to comply. If the chairman feels strongly about a directive, the administration may back down and compromise, or it even may observe the letter of the language. However, if the administrator is determined, high-ranking officials in the secretary's office will contact the chairman. Of course, agencies take more liberties with committee chairmen who are "the nice old men type who do not take it out of our hide." On the other hand, Chairman Rooney of the State Department Committee has the reputation of being a dangerous man to ignore regardless of whether he is advised beforehand.

The type of sanction the committee chooses depends on several variables.[41] If it wants to set an example for other agencies to see and to shun, the punitive proviso or a reduction in funds will usually be employed. These same drastic sanctions are used when an agency has a history of ignoring nonstatutory controls. If the agency, however, rarely fails to comply, it may be subjected to nothing more than a verbal rebuke. The magnitude of the offense—the amount transferred to an activity deleted in the report—is also an important variable.

An agency that disregards several report directives risks more than a sanction for each incident. Research by Ira

39. 109 *Congressional Record* 13376-79 (1963). See also Wildavsky, *Politics of the Budgetary Process*, p. 77.
40. Wildavsky, *Politics of the Budgetary Process*, p. 76.
41. If the executive disregards the committee report, the appropriations committee can insert the same language in the act. This form of sanction usually ensures that the executive will implement the committee's views. For example see House Report (86-1592), pp. 13-15, with regard to cotton reclassing.

Sharkansky reveals that agency response to nonstatutory guidance is a crucial factor in determining the subcommittee's "overall severity of supervision and control."[42]

To determine the rank of four Health, Education and Welfare agencies with respect to the "severity of subcommittee supervision" Sharkansky measured: (1) subcommittee attention through number of questions asked each agency, (2) subcommittee thoroughness through percentage of items receiving "minimum coverage," (3) subcommittee incisiveness through requests for cost justifications, (4) independence of supervision through ratio of questions asked department (as opposed to agency) witnesses, (5) reductions or increases in expenditures, and (6) number of directives in reports. A key reason that the Office of Education receives greater attention than the other three agencies resulted from its record of being "more adventurous" in its disregard of report directives.

AREAS IN WHICH NONSTATUTORY TECHNIQUES ARE
LEAST EFFECTIVE

The effectiveness of nonstatutory techniques diminishes greatly when they are employed to control policy or procedure formulated primarily by the Bureau of the Budget and the White House. This diminished impact is especially evident with respect to "administration policy" in a broad program area—such as health or agriculture—or program guidelines that apply to several departments.

Throughout the Eisenhower administration the agriculture reports included sweeping indictments of the administration's general approach to the farm problem. "Unless present programs are reversed they will wreck farm power and eventually the entire economy."[43] Such exhortations did not deter the administration from continuing the same policy.

The Public Works Subcommittees in several reports protested the Eisenhower administration's policy of "no new

42. Ira Sharkansky, "An Appropriations Subcommittee and Its Client Agencies," *American Political Science Review*, 59 (1965), pp. 622-27.
43. House Report (86-1592), p. 9.

starts" but did not manage to get one proposed new project in a budget request.[44] The Public Works Subcommittees could not cut the budget for the White House or Executive Office of the President and thus had no way to influence policy makers who determined there would be "no new starts." In a similar case, the State Department backed by a presidential determination ignored a restriction on expenses for the Congo.[45]

The departments protect themselves by "passing the buck" to the White House. In the 1950's the Agriculture Department refused to sell cotton overseas at competitive prices in spite of repeated report directives. This refusal originated at the Cabinet level, because competitive sales would have had an adverse impact on foreign policy. The Agriculture Department avoided an appropriations sanction by contending it was unable to implement the appropriations directive because of a Cabinet decision.

Each of the five subcommittees at some point attempted to use nonstatutory techniques to reverse Budget Bureau policy that was publicly supported by the President. The outcome of their efforts was uniform—complete failure. For instance, the Budget Bureau's ability to impound the funds frustrated the Labor—Health, Education and Welfare Subcommittee's attempt to initiate several health programs. "The Committee *directs* the Secretary of Health, Education and Welfare to keep it fully informed as to the apportionment of funds made available for National Institutes of Health programs, with particular emphasis on reporting delays in apportionment. And the committee admonishes the executive branch not to use the apportionment device willfully to thwart the evident conviction of Congress and of the American people that medical research shall move forward on broad fronts."[46]

This does not mean, however, the Budget Bureau is indif-

44. Senate Report (86-486), pp. 2-4.
45. Senate Hearings in State Department Appropriations for 1962 (87-1), p. 173.
46. Senate Report (86-425), p. 25. Emphasis added.

ferent to an agency's need to maintain good relations with Congress. A strong statement in the appropriations committee report is sometimes a justification with the Budget Bureau for allocation of funds to certain programs.

At times appropriations reports urge more emphasis on a program in the next budget request. The Budget Bureau, however, will sometimes cut increases based on such report comments.[47] As a Labor Department official pointed out to irate Congressmen: "We requested the Budget Bureau to give us the money. The Budget Bureau cut us. Our request went over there according to the committee's views, but the Budget Bureau gave us $100,000 for migratory labor and took $43,000 out of safety."[48]

As a staff arm of the President, the Budget Bureau is not within the jurisdiction of the Labor—Health, Education and Welfare Subcommittee, and consequently the subcommittee sanctions are ineffective. Hubert Humphrey, at that time senator (D.-Minn.), accurately sums up the appropriations committees' experience with nonstatutory controls and the Budget Bureau: "I fully agree with the Senator that if language in the report is made a part of the conference committee report by both Houses, it will exercise *some control*, because as I understand the language would be directed to the TVA Board. The TVA Board is an instrumentality under the direction of Congress. I am willing to trust the TVA Board. If the language were directed to the AEC or Budget Bureau, I would feel that the language was worth only about as much as the lines on the paper. . . ."[49]

As Senator Humphrey indicates, certain agencies like the Atomic Energy Commission are largely immune to appropriations sanctions. This immunity depends on the degree of protection the AEC can gather from several sources—the urgency

47. Indeed Budget Bureau examiners cull the appropriations reports for such directives and give requests based on committee recommendations a special review.

48. Senate Hearings on Labor Department Appropriations for 1955 (83-2), p. 80.

49. 101 *Congressional Record* 9863 (1955). Emphasis added.

of the program, the degree of support from public opinion and the legislative committee, the influence of interest group allies, and the agency's general reputation for honesty and efficiency.[50]

Professor Morgan Thomas concludes that the Atomic Energy Commission's unusual capacity to avoid sanctions stemmed mainly from the urgency of the arms race. In the 1950's the Atomic Energy Program was considered an emergency program, and the Joint Committee on Atomic Energy stressed the dire effects of any attempt to reduce AEC funds. When the JCAE protested that a cut or a proviso hindered the arms race, their arguments could not be dismissed lightly. The unusually close JCAE-AEC relationship provided a bulwark against the actions of the appropriations committee.[51] However, any "crash program" such as space or defense might enjoy similar protection.

50. See Thomas, "Appropriations Control and the Atomic Energy Commission," p. 158.

51. See Harold Green and Alan Rosenthal, *Government of the Atom* (New York: Atherton Press, 1963), for an analysis of this unique relationship.

# IV. *Why the Appropriations Committees Employ Nonstatutory Techniques*

INTRODUCTION

There are many areas of policy and administration the appropriations committees want to control but where statutory regulations would be impossible or inappropriate. Indeed the main impetus for extralegal devices is derived from their immunity from a point of order. Such controls can be employed where Congressional rules prohibit statutory regulations.[1] Moreover, statutory provisos that attach conditions to the expenditures of funds cannot be adapted to many situations the committee wants to control. In short, nonstatutory devices have a unique role to play in Congressional oversight—a role that no other technique is capable of filling.[2]

In addition to this unique role Congress often prefers to use nonstatutory techniques even where statutory regulation is feasible. Evidence of this preference for nonstatutory controls is compiled mainly from interviews with appropriations committee members and committee staff. Nevertheless, there are examples in the hearings as Professor Huzer observes in *The Purse and the Sword*: "Even so, the expenditure of public funds for military purposes is not 'foot loose and fancy free.' Many controls which might have been included in the statute are contained, instead, in understandings between members of the Appropriations Committees and officials of the Defense Department. . . . An officer suggesting some statutory language was once interrupted by a Senator who said, 'Well, I do not think it is necessary to put in those words. If we just in-

1. This assertion is based in part on the unanimous responses of House and Senate Appropriations Committee members and their staffs.
2. A subsequent section of this chapter will demonstrate the high frequency of nonstatutory techniques.

creased the amount and earmarked it in the report, I think it would be all right."[3]

If committee members think an agency will probably comply with nonstatutory language, many times they decide *not* to include a specific requirement in the act.[4] As one senator remarked, "If we have an understanding in the record, then I will not press an amendment. Otherwise I think it would be justified to take such steps as necessary."[5]

RULES PROHIBITING LEGISLATION
IN AN APPROPRIATIONS ACT

The precise legal boundaries between legislative committees and appropriations committees is complicated. Friction and usurpation are inherent in a situation in which largely parallel sets of committees vie for control over policy and administrative management. The whole distinction between the jurisdiction of the two committees rests on provisions in the rules of the chambers which are enforced by points of order that can be made on the floor by any member. Basically, authorizing bills (from the legislative committees) may not appropriate funds, and appropriations bills (from the appropriations committees) may not include legislation.

The lines of demarcation remain blurred, however, in spite of years of interpretative decisions. Even though the rules of both Houses forbid legislation in appropriations bills, provisions of a clearly legislative nature slip through both Houses without being challenged, through either inattention or comity. In addition, if the House Committee on Appropriations wants to legislate, it can sometimes obtain a special rule from the rules committee waiving points of order against the bill (though this rule must be agreed to by a two-thirds vote of the House members voting during floor consideration).

3. Elias Huzar, *The Purse and the Sword: Control of the Army by Congress through Military Appropriations* (Ithaca: Cornell University Press, 1950), p. 355.

4. All members of Congress and committee staff interviewed agreed with this view.

5. Huzar, *The Purse and the Sword*, p. 355.

Despite loopholes in the rule prohibiting legislation in an appropriations bill, the threat of a point of order deters legislative attempts by the appropriations committees. Of course, points of order in many cases are sustained, and many precedents are clear.[6]

The main restriction on the jurisdiction of the appropriations committees is that they cannot direct the executive to do anything or to initiate a program, unless it has been authorized by law. In addition, any provision in an appropriations bill changing existing law, adding to it, or repealing it is also out of order.

Even in cases in which the authorizing legislation appears to leave discretion, propositions in appropriation bills that contain *affirmative* directions for executive officers are subject to a point of order.[7] Furthermore, limitations in appropriations acts must not impose new duties on an administrator, unless they provide that no part or only a fraction of the appropriations under consideration shall be used for a designated purpose.[8] The appropriations committees are able to restrict executive discretion insofar as this can be done by a simple negative on the use of the appropriations.

The result of these several rulings is that the appropriations committee can legally employ the statute in a negative manner but not in a positive manner. It is out of order to tell the administrator to do something, but the rules permit the appropriations committees to instruct an administrator not to do something.

The significant effects of the prohibition against affirmative actions can best be illustrated by some of the precedent making decisions. The House Appropriations Committee in a 1907 naval appropriations bill included a proviso that "no part of said money shall be expended until a test shall be

6. The writer has no knowledge of "point of order" language being eliminated in the Senate. The differences between the House and Senate in this respect deserve further research.

7. Lewis Deschler, *Rules of the House of Representatives* (Washington: Government Printing Office, 1961), p. 432.

8. *Ibid.*, pp. 433-44.

made with a service 12″ projectile fired against a 12″ Krupp-ized armor plate at a range of 5,000 yards to ascertain whether a projectile will penetrate the armor plate."[9] Note that the committee was trying to phrase essentially positive instructions in negative terms to avoid a point of order. However, the chair ruled it out of order because the amendment implied that the Secretary of Navy must do certain things before he gets the money.

A proviso was inserted in 1907 to require the Government Printing Office to follow rules of orthography established by Webster or other generally accepted dictionaries. The chair ruled: "A provision authorizing or directing an officer of the Government to do things involves legislation. The language of this statute requires the Public Printer hereafter to pursue a particular line of action or do things. It has been held . . . a paragraph proposing a construction of law different from that adhered to by the Department was legislation and not a limitation."[10]

A 1902 provision directing the secretary of war to consolidate the existing commissions in charge of various military parks was ruled out of order on the basis that it directed the secretary "to do certain things."[11] A similar case involved a requirement that no money be expended on supplies for the Army except those orders specifying delivery at a convenient point. The chair stated: "A limitation, to be in order, must be in effect simply a negative bar pressing upon the appropriation of money, and that any amendment which, directly or indirectly, imposes upon any officer a duty in the expenditure of the money is obnoxious to the point of order. . . . The effect [of the directive in question] is to provide a form of contract. There is certainly more of an affirmative requirement than limitation in the amendment."[12]

9. Asher C. Hinds, *Precedents of the House of Representatives of the United States* (Washington: Government Printing Office, 1907), Vol. IV, #3475.

10. Hinds, Vol. IV, #3854.

11. *Ibid.*, #3859.

12. Clarence Cannon, *Precendents of House of Representatives* (Washington: Government Printing Office, 1953), p. 1678.

Negative instructions in the statute are also subject to certain limitations. Thus, a House precedent states that a proviso to restrict executive discretion to a degree that may be fairly termed a change in policy, rather than a matter of administrative detail, is out of order.[13] In addition no appropriations act can take away authority or discretion conferred by law.[14]

There is some flexibility in these restrictions on the appropriations committee. Of particular importance is the ruling that the object to be appropriated for may be described in detail without violating the rules.[15] Another significant factor is that clauses effecting a retrenchment of expenditures are not out of order.[16] Retrenchment is defined liberally by the rules, but the reduction must be certain not just probable.[17]

APPROPRIATIONS COMMITTEES TAKE THE INITIATIVE

Although the appropriations committees typically reduce and limit existing government programs, they occasionally seek to initiate new programs; and here, as one would expect, they run up against the rules relating to appropriations bills. Frequently, the programs that are initiated in committee reports have never been authorized. Moreover, affirmative directions in appropriations bills are out of order, and it is almost impossible to initiate a program or policy in negative form.

Program initiation by appropriations committees is a very important dimension of the unique role of nonstatutory controls. For example, in 1960, the House Labor–Health, Education and Welfare report outlined a wide-ranging accident prevention program. "On the basis of information submitted to the Committee in the Surgeon General's report such a [accident prevention] program should include a national data

13. Deshler, *Rules of the House of Representatives*, p. 434.
14. *Ibid.*, p. 432.
15. *Ibid.*, p. 432.
16. Hinds, *Precedents of the House of Representatives*, #3864.
17. Floyd Riddick, *The United States Congress Organization and Procedure* (Manassas, Virginia: National Capitol Publishers, Inc., 1949), p. 285.

collection and evaluation system, a comprehensive research program . . . a vigorous effort to demonstrate tested control procedures."[18] Since this accident prevention program was not authorized, it could not be included in the appropriations act.

Another frequent objective of appropriations initiative is the formal organization of the executive branch. Since the legislative committees have jurisdiction over organizational structure, the appropriations committees must employ nonstatutory techniques. In view of the necessary relationship between executive organization and efficient and effective administration, the appropriations committees have not hesitated to use their reports as a mechanism for wide-ranging reorganizations.

After the Republicans gained control of Congress in 1952, several subcommittees desired extensive changes in agency organizational structure. The House Interior Subcommittee informed the Bonneville Power administration that it "is under the impression that the entire program of decentralization should be reviewed and office consolidations made."[19] This same report concluded with a statement that the committee had grave doubts about the desirability of widespread regionalization in several Interior Department subdivisions and expected a complete study.[20]

Some appropriations subcommittees are not always willing to wait for an agency to reorganize itself. The Labor–Health, Education and Welfare Subcommittees, by voting large increases over the budget requests, were responsible for the phenomenal growth of National Institutes of Health. As this rapid expansion proceeded, it became necessary for the subcommittees to implement without delay the corresponding organizational structure. ". . . the work of these clinical cooperative groups, originally set up under the Research Grants

18. House Report (87-1125), p. 34.
19. 107 *Congressional Record*, 19157 (1961). A subsequent chapter will evaluate this infringement on the jurisdiction of the legislative committee through nonstatutory techniques.
20. *House Report* (86-1428), pp. 13-14.

Division, has reached such a size and stability in organizational pattern that more rapid progress in these clinical centers will be achieved if these activities can be administered as a whole. To achieve these ends the committee adds $1 million for programmed grants *and places* the administration of these grants in the Cancer Chemotherapy National Center."[21]

If the appropriations committees make specific proposals for new programs or organizations in the report, they are often confronted with angry protests on the floor by legislative committee members. An alternative procedure is to urge the executive to devise specific proposals to solve a problem and then submit them to the appropriations subcommittee for approval. Since the appropriations report language is a general prod for policy initiation, legislative committee members cannot point to any specific unauthorized program in the report directive.

This procedure has another important advantage. Appropriations committee members realize that their limited staff resources pose substantial obstacles to initiation of complex programs. The early stages of the legislative process are largely concerned with reducing alternatives, focusing on the more promising possibilities, and ensuring that policy proposals are co-ordinated and consistent.[22] A reduction of alternative proposals requires a large amount of technical information. Effective co-ordination necessarily entails central direction of the policy formulation process. The executive is better able to fulfill both of these functions than an appropriations subcommittee with its small staff (usually one or two professionals). Therefore, rather than outlining a new program in the bill, the subcommittee usually prefers to use statements in the reports that urge a reluctant executive to initiate complicated programs.

The [House Labor–Health, Education and Welfare] committee was likewise again disappointed this

21. Senate Report (86-435), p. 22. Emphasis added.
22. See Arthur Maas and others, *Design of Water-Resource Systems* (Cambridge: Harvard University Press, 1962), pp. 576-81.

year that the Department made such a poor showing
so far as accomplishments are concerned with respect
to the problems of the aging. Since it is well recognized
that this is a growing problem with the steady increase
in the number of older people in our population, it has
been a source of considerable concern on the part of
the committee that so little in the way of a program in
this field could be presented by the Department or
its many constituents whose activities naturally come
in contact with this program. It is certainly to be hoped
that in another year something substantial, in the way
of a program, will be developed.[23]

While the above language does not add to or change existing law, it is definitely an affirmative directive, and if it had
been included in some form in the bill, it could have been
ruled out as legislation. It is permissable to describe the object the committee is appropriating for, but in this case the
committee was not sure what a program for the aged should
include.

In 1957 the Senate Interior Subcommittee asserted that
our national parks were poorly maintained. The subcommittee believed that the predicted large increase in tourism
meant facilities and exhibits should be expanded rapidly. In
light of the refusal of the Eisenhower administration to act,
the Senate report prodded: "The committee has recommended
funds to initiate a long-range program for the improvement
of national parks. It is the view of the committee that the
Forest Service should present a program of this nature and
that funds to implement such a program should be submitted
to the Budget Bureau. . . ."[24] Note that this report language
was a positive directive to an administrator and hence in
statutory form would be subject to a point of order.

A prevalent nonstatutory technique to initiate a program
is simply to request an agency report on solutions to a problem. The subcommittee then holds hearings on the report,
goes over the various approaches with the agency, and di-

23. 102 *Congressional Record* 3451 (1956), reprint of House Report.
24. 104 *Congressional Record* 7713 (1958).

rects certain administrative actions based on the discussions and report.

> In the spring of 1959 [in its report] the House Appropriations Committee requested the National Institute of Mental Health to collaborate with the Children's Bureau in preparing a comprehensive report for the Congress on juvenile delinquency. This report was submitted in February 1960, and a special hearing before the Labor–Health, Education and Welfare Subcommittee of the House took place in March to deal solely with the juvenile delinquency report.
>
> As a result of the report and the hearing the House Committee on Appropriations directed the National Institute of Mental Health to earmark $1 million of the increased funds . . . for the purpose of undertaking new programs and activities aimed at solving the problem of delinquency. Both the House and Senate Appropriations Committees' reports on the fiscal year 1961 budget request indicated that additional funds for consultative services and research in juvenile delinquency were allowed the Children's Bureau.[25]

A request for a study compels a department to turn its attention to the problem but allows it to formulate its own solution. The House Defense Subcommittee approached the perennial controversy over the emphasis on public or private shipyards in its 1963 report:

> The Committee does not fully endorse the position taken by the representatives of private shipbuilding interests . . . that the vast majority of the repair, alteration and conversion work in this program be channeled into private yards. Nor does it fully agree with the Navy that the present method used to allocate work to public yards rather than private yards is proper.
> The entire problem of the utilization of shipyard

25. Statement by Mrs. Katherine B. Oettinger, chief, Children's Bureau, during House Hearings on Labor–Health, Education and Welfare Appropriations for 1962 (87-1), p. 612. No program for juvenile delinquency was authorized.

facilities is a matter for intensive study by the Department of Defense and the Navy with a view toward working out a realistic, practical, and economical approach to the utilization of this capability in a manner commensurate with the best interests of the government. The Committee will expect the Secretary of Defense to cause such a study to be made and the results thereof made available to the Committees on Appropriations of the House of Representatives and of the Senate prior to the consideration of the fiscal year 1964 budget estimates.[26]

The Defense Department is granted freedom of action to propose whatever system it finds to be "realistic, practical, and economical"; but it is informed that any solution will be reviewed by the appropriations committees. This is a good example of the way the committees can try to retain some policy initiative despite their lack of adequate information-gathering resources. By yielding the initial formulation of policies to the executive branch, the committee is able to retain for itself both the ability to choose between the alternatives presented and the initiative in defining the area in which its choice is to be made. The rules, however, preclude affirmative language in the appropriations statute to accomplish these objectives.

At times the committee details the objectives, procedures, and elements of a new program in the report. Such specific recommendations are often based on expert testimony from interested persons and organizations. In the 86th Congress Dr. Sidney Farber of Harvard and Dr. Michael Debakey of Baylor convinced the Senate Labor–Health, Education and Welfare Subcommittee that National Institutes of Health required a number of centralized research clinics. These clinics could supply the highly specialized facilities that a single researcher could not afford. NIH had not studied the uses of such clinics, so the appropriations committee decided to be specific.

26. House Report (87-1607), p. 38.

Such centers should represent the highest achievement in clinical investigation supported by laboratories such as those of pharmacology, chemistry, biology . . . and clinical research facilities such as metabolic wards. They should include among their functions . . . the creation of expert facilities for rapid and accurate evaluation—1) of new anticancer agents, or other methods of treatment; 2) of the efficacy of techniques of vaccination or immunization. These centers should be situated within proximity of already existing universities or research institutions. . . .[27]

A statutory proviso with this purpose could be ruled out of order as an affirmative direction or because such clinical research centers were never authorized.[28]

In many cases, nonstatutory techniques facilitate co-operation between appropriations and legislative committees. The annual appropriations review of administrative performance is usually more frequent than the legislative committee review. Consequently, the appropriations subcommittees discover problems requiring a legislative solution before the legislative committees are cognizant of them. Frequently, the appropriations committees defer to the jurisdictional rights of the legislative committee, but appropriations reports call attention to the problems requiring legislation.

For example, in fiscal 1958 the Senate State Department Subcommittee strongly objected to what it believed was an overlap and duplication of functions between the United States Information Agency and other agencies. Accordingly, the subcommittee stated: "The committee feels strongly that there would be considerable economy and efficiency achieved were the Agency [USIA] returned to the State Department, and unanimously recommends that the Foreign Relations Committee consider legislation providing for the transfer of USIA to the Department of State."[29]

27. Senate Report (86-425), p. 29.
28. A National Institutes of Health officer assured the writer these clinical research centers were not authorized.
29. Senate Report (85-303), p. 9.

Another method for an appropriations subcommittee to bring about new legislation is to work through a friendly executive agency. "The last few years the committee has been impressed with the increasing problem of water supply for domestic and industrial uses. . . . The Chief of [Army] Engineers should review the present authorities available . . . with a view to determining whether any modification of existing legislation is necessary to facilitate the development of water supply potentialities in federally constructed reservoirs."[30]

The unique role of nonstatutory controls is evidenced in both of these situations. Provisos that attach conditions to expenditures cannot be employed to urge a legislative committee to take action. A proviso instructing the executive to request new legislative authority could be ruled out of order as an affirmative direction.

### CIRCUMVENTING POINTS OF ORDER

Statutory provisos must be negative regulations that state "no part or a fraction of the funds" are to be used for a certain activity or project. The following report language pertains to payments to state extension services for agricultural research: "The Secretary is urged to institute a stronger and more thorough review of research programs under this heading in order to curtail duplication of effort and eliminate less essential work."[31]

There seems to be no way the appropriations committee can phrase a proviso in a negative form and still express the same general objective. The same can be said for this excerpt: "Some of the unfortunate incidents which have occurred abroad in connection with cultural exchange presentations indicate that a lack of mature judgement has been used in the selection of certain performing individuals and groups. More care in their selection must be exercised in the future."[32]

30. Senate Report (84-700), p. 13. Emphasis added.
31. House Report (84-303), p. 13.
32. House Report (86-1996), p. 8.

Another example of a positive directive that is feasible for inclusion in a report, but not in the statute, appears in this 1961 agriculture appropriations report. "In connection with new loans, the REA should determine a proper level of reserve for each applicant, should set up criteria for granting new loans, and should make certain that funds are used for the purpose for which they are made available."[33]

At times related programs grow without any thought being given to a general policy or uniform approach. Appropriations subcommittees find themselves unable to make decisions on individual fund requests without some basic policy guides and general criteria. In the 1950's the Corps of Engineers began to construct recreation facilities at a large number of their water projects. With regard to this trend, the House report observed:

> There has been no general policy or uniform approach to the matter of concessions and land-leasing in reservoir areas and of parking fees. . . .
> It is the Committee's recommendation that the proper legislative committees interest themselves in the problem of evolving some sort of national policy to put this growing problem under control. In the meantime the committee requires a full report from both the Corps of Engineers and the Bureau of Reclamation . . . in setting out in detail just what facilities it is contemplated the Federal Government will supply, how the leasing of land and concessions will be handled, and specific guidelines for transferring the management of reservoir areas to the states.
> . . . However, without at least basic policy guides the Committee finds itself in a very difficult position in its review of the fund requests for such facilities on a project-by-project basis.[34]

The appropriations committees have reworded a positive direction so that it is in effect a negative limitation that can

33. House Report (87-448), p. 27. Agriculture Department employees assured the writer this directive would be ruled out of order.
34. House Report (86-1634), p. 3.

be included in the statute. The classic example of this practice appears in a 1907 naval appropriations bill. The original proviso read: ". . . that before construction of these vessels shall be begun a test shall be made with a service 12″ projectile fired against a 12″ Kruppized armor plate at a range of 5,000 yards to ascertain whether such projectile . . . will penetrate such armor plate."[35] This proviso was excluded because it was an affirmative direction. The amendment was rephrased so "that no part of said money shall be expended until a test shall be made to ascertain. . . ."[36] Again the chair ruled it out of order because the amendment implied that the secretary of Navy must do certain things before he received the money. Consequently, the amendment was offered in this form: "Provided, that no part of said sum shall be expended for any armor plate that has not been subjected to test showing said armor plate cannot be penetrated by a 12″ service gun. . . ."[37] This time the presiding officer ruled the amendment did not violate the rules.

While this rewording process can accomplish some positive objectives of the appropriations committee, many affirmative directives cannot be effectively rephrased.[38] For instance, the House committee would not have been able to reword the positive instructions to the Rural Electrification Administration or to the Corps of Engineers in the preceding examples and still accomplish its objective. Consequently, the appropriations committee had no choice but to employ nonstatutory techniques.

In some situations appropriations subcommittees want to exercise a modified legislative veto over administrative actions. Yet any attempt to establish such a procedure through

35. Hinds, *Precedents of the House of Representatives,* Vol. IV, #3975.
36. *Ibid.*
37. *Ibid.*
38. As a proviso is reworded its original meaning may be distorted. A possible drawback to this procedure is that the slightly different meaning of the acceptable version may hinder administrative flexibility to a greater extent than the original form. The need for administrative flexibility will be discussed below.

the statute could be ruled out of order.[39] Therefore, the sub-committee utilizes the report or the hearings to institute a modified legislative veto whereby the administration must inform the subcommittee of a decision immediately before or after it has been reached. This is not a general progress re-port, but rather provides a specific opportunity for the ap-propriations subcommittee to overrule executive decisions.

For example, the Rural Electrification Administration noti-fies every member of both the Senate and House Agriculture Subcommittee upon the *receipt or approval* of each specific generation and transmission loan. When a loan is approved the subcommittees are informed of the criteria used in this particular decision.[40] A procedure similar to the REA case is used by the interior subcommittee to regulate overseas forest research. The Interior Department must notify the appropriations subcommittees prior to undertaking forest re-search in any foreign country other than Canada.[41]

Any provision in an appropriations bill proposing to con-strue existing law is in itself a proposition of legislation and therefore not in order.[42] However, the appropriations com-mittees evade this ruling by including in their reports lengthy interpretations of the authorizing statute. In 1963 the Interior Department claimed the Alaskan Statehood Act indicated land survey areas should be fifty thousand acres in size. Alaska contended ten thousand acres was the correct inter-pretation of the legislative history, but the Interior Depart-ment opposed this tremendous decrease in survey require-ments. The Senate Interior Subcommittee ruled in favor of Alaska:

A reading of the statute and committee reports on the legislation which was enacted into law leads to the

39. See Cannon, *Precedents of the House of Representatives*, p. 1691 for basis of this statement.
40. Senate Hearings on Agriculture Appropriations for 1963 (87-2), p. 34.
41. House Hearings on Interior Appropriations for 1956 (84-1), p. 681.
42. Hinds, IV, #3936-38.

clear and definite conclusion that Congress intended that so long as the State selections meet the specifically stated requirements of the act there should be an exterior boundary survey of each land selection made by the State of Alaska.

Therefore, the committee *directs* that the Secretary of Interior cause surveys of Alaskan land selections made under the terms of P.L. 85-508 to be executed in compliance with this report [which supported Alaska's position].[43]

It is such an accepted practice for appropriations committees to interpret legislative authority in the reports that the administration will sometimes ask for guidance. The following report comment is in response to an inquiry by the Corps of Engineers. "The committee is of the opinion that the Corps of Engineers has too narrowly and conservatively interpreted their authority for bank stabilization work on the Red River."[44]

CONGRESSIONAL WARNINGS AND REBUKES

The use of the appropriations report to issue warnings and rebukes to the executive branch stems in part from the point-of-order rule. Any attempt to include a warning or a rebuke in the bill would constitute legislation and be ruled out of order. Further, warnings and rebukes do not fit the traditional pattern of appropriations statutes that attach conditions to expenditures.

The hearings provide an excellent opportunity to convey dissatisfaction. The reports are utilized if the committee wants to insure that the administrator's superiors are aware of the criticism and to impart a feeling of urgency.

There are numerous report comments that attack inefficiency, lethargy, stupidity, bias, and poorly presented testimony. In 1958 the House Labor—Health, Education and

43. Senate Report (88-181), pp. 3-4. Emphasis added.
44. Senate Report (85-609), p. 19.

Welfare Committee reproached the Indian Health Bureau for several of these reasons:

> While there is no doubt that good has been accomplished with the increased funds, the administration of this program [Indian Health] leaves much to be desired.
>
> . . . Congress appropriated funds for construction of a new hospital . . . over 2-1/2 years ago. The details of the fumbling around on this project are set forth in the hearings on pages 297-301.
>
> . . . The Committee is at a complete loss to understand why with this big increase, the Public Health Service has not been able to reopen the closed ward at the Fort Defiance Hospital.
>
> . . . The other three hospitals for which funds were appropriated are in the same status—plans still have not progressed to the point where they can be submitted to Budget Bureau for approval.
>
> The Committee will expect the Secretary to take a personal interest in correcting the administrative shortcomings.[45]

Such a stinging rebuke by the House will ensure a follow-through by the Senate. In this case, the Senate demanded that the Indian Health Bureau present specific measures that would rectify the situations criticized by the House.[46]

The following report excerpt is an excellent example of the unique role of nonstatutory guidance. This criticism of the Joint Chiefs of Staff is aimed at fundamental changes in the system of military policy formulation.

> It seems quite apparent that . . . the Joint Chiefs of Staff, as a corporate body, is not providing the kind of advice and leadership which this country requires.
> The individual members of the Joint Chiefs of Staff

45. House Report (85-1645), p. 16. Chairman Jensen exposed many of these shortcomings on his field trip.
46. Senate Hearings on Labor—Health, Education and Welfare Appropriations for 1959 (85-2), p. 638. At the end of his presentation the administrator remarked, "I think we can show you some remarkable progress next year."

are able and experienced military men. It is not with these individuals but rather with the organization and system of operations that the Committee is concerned. . . . The President, the Secretary of Defense, the Congress, and the American people have a right to expect a better job from the Joint Chiefs of Staff in the way of military guidance. As a corporate body, the Joint Chiefs of Staff must set up plans for the guidance of the various commands and the respective services. Hard decisions are required, and the President, the Secretary of Defense and the Joint Chiefs must assume the major responsibility for tailoring military forces to requirements. Each year the question which confronts us of who gets what is becoming more difficult to cope with.

The Joint Chiefs of Staff should look at what is available for what purposes and attempt to match it with the needs. As an example, the Joint Chiefs should take a look at the combined forces of the Marine Corps and the Army. It is not a question of combining the Army and Marine Corps. It is merely a question of looking at the combined strength and the combined capability of these two great forces in making the final determination as to what our ground force should be in providing for our commitments throughout the world. . . . Such an approach should be the function of the Joint Chiefs of Staff in connection with preparation of plans for the 1961 budget request. The costing out of such determinations can be done by the respective services and through the usual budgetary process.

Many of the basic military questions which confront the Congress and the country are apparently never discussed by the Joint Chiefs of Staff. For example, the hearings reveal that the Joint Chiefs did not discuss specifically in connection with the 1960 military budget whether the Army should be maintained at 870,000 or 900,000, whether funds should be sought for a Navy carrier, and what should be done with reference to the B-52 bomber program.[47]

47. House Report (86-408), pp. 10-11.

A rebuke in the report provides an effective way for the committee to draw a common error to the attention of many agencies. In 1958 the House Public Works Subcommittee criticized the Corps of Engineers for behavior that could apply to many agencies that assist local projects. "The Committee has noted the evident super-salesmanship on the part of some Corps of Engineers personnel in whipping up local enthusiasm for projects which from the standpoint of local contributions and other aspects should never be recommended favorable to Congress. The Committee does not regard extra-curricular activities of this type as being either in the line of duty or as constructive contributions. . . ."[48]

The reports and hearings include various types of warnings that the subcommittees hope will forestall the need for more formal restrictions. Often a warning is strengthened by an intimation of stringent limitations that will follow if the warning is not heeded.

> The committee *expects* the [State] Department to make every effort to reduce the number of [international] organizations to which we contribute in order to avoid duplication and waste and also to obtain reductions in the amounts we are requested to contribute. Reductions in our percentage of contribution are not sufficient if the over-all budgets of these organizations are allowed to increase. Unless additional results are forthcoming, stringent limitations can be expected.[49]

At times a subcommittee wants to guard against actions or developments that might occur, but are not at present amenable to statutory control.

> The [House Agriculture] committee is disturbed by evidence of efforts to gradually eliminate this [Soil Conservation] program. Apparently a task force of the Commission of Intergovernmental Relations intends to recommend that this organization and its work be

48. House Report (85-1864), p. 11.
49. House Report (83-341), p. 4. Emphasis added.

turned over to the state extension services. . . . Certain factors tend to indicate some sympathy within the Department and Budget Bureau for the reported position of the Commission. . . . It is requested that the committee be notified by the Department as soon as official recommendations are received from the Commission. . . .

The committee is firmly opposed to the subordination of the Soil Conservation Service to any other agency.[50]

It was not feasible to include such a warning in a proviso that attaches conditions to the expenditure of funds. The report, however, can alert the administrator to the appropriations committee's adamant opposition and thus serve as a deterrent.[51]

RECONCILING ADMINISTRATIVE FLEXIBILITY
AND APPROPRIATIONS CONTROL

In some situations legal restrictions present the appropriations committees with a choice between unduly hampering administrative flexibility or sacrificing appropriations influence over important policy. Part of this conflict is caused by the rule prohibiting legislation in an appropriations act. Most statutory appropriations provisions that are phrased to allow flexibility constitute legislation.

Nonstatutory techniques enable the appropriations committees to reconcile a measure of administrative discretion with appropriations control. For instance, nonstatutory devices that can be disregarded in unforeseen circumstances allow administrators who are more familiar with conditions in the field to adapt law enforcement to changing situations. These techniques facilitate administration of the law by not freezing into the statute provisions that are workable in some contexts and unworkable in others. Yet they permit Congress

50. House Report (84-303), pp. 15-16.
51. For a similar example see House Report (83-1756), pp. 13-14.

to exert a considerable degree of influence over administrative performance.

In 1947 the House Agriculture Subcommittee thought departmental publicity expenditures were excessive and wanted to insert a proviso limiting man years for publicity work. Statutory control, however, could not be used without completely disrupting the information job of the department. The subcommittees reluctantly concluded: ". . . it was found all but impossible to draft a provision in such terms as would not endanger the fundamental work of the Department in diffusing essential information. . . . The committee believes it is a matter which can be controlled by the more flexible device of administrative regulations . . . and the Department should be able to achieve the purpose of the Committee."[52]

There are several types of situations that require flexible nonstatutory devices. For instance, flexibility is essential during delicate negotiations surrounding an important contract between the federal government and other public bodies, or between government and private organizations. Extralegal techniques can be employed to express the committees' attitude on the settlement the negotiations should reach, some of the criteria that should be considered, and even specific clauses that must be included. While the administrator will consider the sentiments of the powerful appropriations committee so that he can compromise the committee's views in order to successfully conclude negotiations, any attempt to establish a statutory standard permitting administrative discretion would constitute legislation in an appropriations act.

Report comments do not require complete agreement by committee members and both Houses on the precise wording. Also nonstatutory language can be skillfully phrased so that it does more than express a Congressional desire that an accommodation be reached. Consider the 1951 Senate report with respect to transmission of power in North Carolina.

The committee, therefore, *directs* the Southeastern Power Administration and the Secretary of Interior

52. House Report (80-450), p. 8.

to exhaust every possible effort to obtain proper wheeling agreements before utilizing the funds recommended for the above-mentioned facilities. It is the hope of the committee that it will not be found necessary to use these funds. . . . In the judgement of the committee, fair and reasonable efforts should be made by the public utility companies in the areas concerned . . . and likewise . . . when fair and reasonable offers are made . . . such offers *should be accepted* by the Secretary of the Interior.[53]

The appropriations committees frequently use reports, hearings, letters, and phone calls to direct and prod forward contract negotiations. At times the committee's recommendations are very specific.

It is the *desire* of the committee that the existing contracts between Southwestern Power Administration and the Government cooperatives become operative immediately upon approval of this act.

*It is the opinion* of the committee that the Secretary should give consideration to amending the contracts as follows:

1. Deletion of the provision giving the Southwestern Power Administration an option to purchase the transmission facilities of the generation and transmission cooperatives. . . .

2. To allow the generation and transmission cooperatives to operate and maintain their facilities. . . .

3. To allow the Southwestern Power Administration and the generation and transmission cooperatives to settle accounts on a net balance basis.[54]

Even though the above report was specific, the Southwestern Power Administration decided the contract the committee recommended was not suitable for some power co-operatives. Accordingly, different arrangements were made that better

53. Senate Report (82-299), p. 4. Emphasis added.
54. Senate Report (84-700), p. 5. Emphasis added—note non-mandate language.

suited the particular circumstances of the various power co-operatives.[55]

These public-private electric power conflicts further illustrate the unique role of nonstatutory techniques for controlling important substantive policy. A particularly noteworthy example concerned the House Public Works Subcommittee's desire to ensure that public groups could participate in the development of nuclear electric power. The subcommittee realized, however, that the final decision on the best research and development proposals must be left to the Atomic Energy Commission. "It is hoped that the door will not be completely shut on the participation of such [public] groups in the nuclear power reactor program, and that the $15,000,000 provided in the bill for research and development on unsolicited proposals *will be considered available* for proposals by public power groups. . . . It is also *expected* that such proposals will be given equal consideration with any which may be made by private utilities."[56]

Nonstatutory techniques are particularly useful in circumstances where the appropriations committee is not certain that a program or action it favors will accomplish the committee's objective. Many times the committee will make a suggestion that it expects the administrator to consider seriously but which can be disregarded if there are compelling reasons.[57]

REP. MAY [R.-Wash.]: On the same page of that report the committee states that it *feels* that the activity of the service for mental retardation under the Office of Education is of such importance that they have made another recommendation that *consideration should be given* to designating an assistant to the Commissioner [of Education] to be in charge of the activity. . . . Would the gentleman enlarge on that specifically. . . .

55. See House Hearings on Public Works Appropriations for 1958 (85-1), p. 548ff.

56. House Report (86-1634), p. 36. Emphasis added.

57. It is interesting to note that legislative committees also use nonstatutory controls in this type of situation.

Rep. Laird [ranking member]: We *feel* that by concentrating responsibility in one person who would devote his entire time to the program . . . that it would be of great help in furthering the program.[58]

Another interesting example of this practice involved the communications satellite: "The Committee urges that the Department of Defense approach this program [the communications satellite] with caution. . . . The Committee feels that when a synchronous orbit satellite system is developed, it will be much superior to the medium altitude random orbit system currently proposed by the department . . . the Committee feels that the deployment of a random orbit system, if a synchronous orbit system might not be too far behind, would not be wise."[59]

The appropriations committee often wants a program intensified or de-emphasized but does not wish to restrict flexibility by specifying a statutory allowance. The committee feels the administrator through daily contact in building up the program is best able to determine the required amount of money.

. . . the Committee urges the furtherance of the rural telephone program by the Rural Electric Administration *in a sound and equitable manner.* . . . The Committee believes that REA should more actively encourage private telephone industry to expand its service into rural areas. There are rural areas which private enterprise cannot or will not serve adequately. . . . It is the consensus of the Committee that REA should advance Federal funds for the provision of the telephone service in rural areas where private enterprise cannot or will not provide adequate service.[60]

To the above should be added the Senate's view. "The Committee urges the REA to move *as fast as consistent with good*

58. 107 *Congressional Record* 8256 (1961). Emphasis added. Notice the use of the word "feels," which means that the committee does not consider its comments mandatory.
59. House Report (88-439), p. 55.
60. House Report (83-422), p. 13. Emphasis added.

*business methods* with its loan and construction programs.
. . . To overcome the delays and slow progress in bringing
service to the large number without telephones, it is urged
that every avenue be pursued."[61]

Many provisos and specifications in the act are intended
to control temporary situations. However, administrators
and congressmen alike complain that it is extremely difficult
to persuade Congressional supporters of a proviso to allow
repeal. One member of the House Appropriations Committee observed bitterly, "Once a proviso gets in the law, it seldom ever gets out." The result is analysed by Professor
Gaus: "Special restrictions were frequently written into the
law to correct a specific abuse . . . but the restriction remained
in the law long after the situation that gave rise to it had
passed. Whatever the merits or the desirability of any one
restrictive measure, in their entirety such measures consti-
tuted an imposing mass of legal entanglements. Certainly
much of the inflexibility, cumbersomeness, and expense of
administration could be traced to that source."[62]

In view of such results, Congress has decided that the administrative flexibility permitted by nonstatutory techniques
is preferable, even when there is no immediate need for such
discretion. Since the committees lack the agencies' technical
insight, they cannot be certain that some rigid statutory requirement will not prove unworkable in future contexts. One
subcommittee clerk explained: "We use nonstatutory controls a lot because we always try to give the Department a
chance to work things out for themselves. We use a proviso
usually only when they have not satisfied our nonstatutory
recommendations. There are many areas where we want to
give the Department flexibility, since we do not have the
expertise to stipulate requirements in a statute."

61. Senate Report (83-382), p. 14. Emphasis added. For administrative response see House Hearings on Agriculture Appropriations
for 1955 (83-2), Part 3, pp. 1184-91.

62. John Gaus and Leon V. Wolcott, *Public Administration and the
United States Department of Agriculture* (Chicago: University of Chicago Press, 1940), p. 434.

Professor Huzar discovered the same attitude within the defense subcommittees: "Actually, Congressmen have usually behaved pretty much as though they were well aware that they are not competent to exercise close control over expenditures of military appropriations, and that effective administration might be impaired if many detailed directions were frozen into the statutes."[63]

This attitude has been carefully cultivated by administrators who prefer nonstatutory controls to rigid statutory restrictions. An Agriculture Department official observed: "We try to bring the committee over to our way of thinking about nonstatutory control. If we have faith in each other, and a good working relationship, they will use more nonstatutory control. We have a close understanding and keep the Agriculture Subcommittee informed if we are going to ignore nonstatutory instruction. We are not as close to the Interior Subcommittee [that handles the Forest Service Budget], so they put more controls in the statute."

### A MORE EFFECTIVE OVERSIGHT TECHNIQUE

In many situations nonstatutory techniques provide more effective and precise Congressional control. Since language in the statute is subject to various interpretations, the agencies, on the basis of their counsel's interpretation, can draw the teeth out of a statutory restriction.[64] Appropriations subcommittees believe that through nonstatutory devices and interim meetings they can enforce not only the letter of their directive but also its spirit. In effect, the subcommittees become the sole judge of adequate compliance. Moreover, since nonstatutory devices can be disregarded in special circumstances, the agency is usually willing to observe the full intent of report language.[65]

63. Huzar, *The Purse and the Sword*, p. 354.
64. See Lucius Wilmerding, Jr., *Spending Power* (New Haven: Yale University Press, 1943), pp. 110-12.
65. Furthermore, the appropriations committees may be reluctant to include in appropriations bills discretionary phrases that do not fit the traditional pattern of mandatory appropriations language.

Some administrators have complained about the increased expense involved in complying with a statutory regulation. In 1956 the House Agriculture Subcommittee included a proviso that specified $500,000 for a study of the methods used by other countries to sell farm commodities in world markets. The agency agreed to undertake the study but protested the use of a proviso. "This language would serve no useful purpose and would require additional expenses to administer the limitation. . . . The language would be expensive and difficult to administer in view of its involving three areas of activity."[66] The department claimed the study entailed additional personnel in three different divisions, and therefore they would have difficulty certifying the expenditure of $500,000. The subcommittee agreed to include the study in a report statement.

Report directives are used because they are less likely to arouse questions during floor debates. One Republican senator remarked, "If you tuck it away in the report there is not much notice taken of it. If you use a proviso it often opens up floor debate from members who watch this sort of thing." A subcommittee staff director stressed that it is more difficult to devise a technical amendment on the floor to offset complicated nonstatutory language than to propose elimination of a statutory proviso.[67]

THE PERFORMANCE BUDGET AND NONSTATUTORY TECHNIQUES

The recommendations of the first Hoover Commission in 1949 provided the impetus for a substantial postwar increase in the use of nonstatutory controls. The commission concluded that fundamental reforms were needed in methods and structure of the appropriations acts. Budgets had been poorly designed with too much emphasis on the expenditure objects.

66. Statement by Earl L. Butz, Assistant Secretary of Agriculture, in Senate Hearings on Agriculture Appropriations for 1956 (84-1), pp. 307-3161.
67. Since a report is not legislation, it is impossible for language in a report to be stricken by an amendment from the floor. An amendment must be so phrased as to offset the language.

The Hoover Commission's key proposal advocated a budget based upon functions, activities, and programs, now commonly termed a performance budget.

The commission also recommended a substantial revision of the government's complicated appropriations structure. The principal objective was to simplify the presentation and thereby make it more meaningful. This was to be accomplished by the consolidation of many small and unimportant appropriation items into broader categories. Thus, the new appropriations structure would eliminate needless itemization that obscured totals and hopefully transform the previously patchwork appropriation procedures into a rational, uniform, and easily understood pattern.[68]

Major revisions were implemented immediately as evidenced by the elimination of over 200 statutory appropriation items in the 1951 budget, and 50 more in 1952. The Budget Bureau continued to refine and simplify the budget, with the result that statutory appropriation items were reduced from 2,000 in 1940 to 375 in 1960.[69]

Congress, and particularly the appropriations committees, co-operated fully in the restructuring of the appropriations statutes. However, in return for less detailed statutory control, the appropriations committees demanded assurances that the agencies would observe the detailed budget presentations. If such assurances were given, Congress felt that the Hoover Commission proposals would facilitate both the measurement and control of costs. A typical pledge was made by former Secretary of the Interior Chapman. "We recognize the authorization of funds under a smaller number of appropriations items places greater responsibility on the Department to control the use of the funds for the purpose for which they are authorized, and in compliance with the directions made

68. A simplified appropriations structure would also make administration less expensive and complex.

69. U.S. Congress, Senate Committee on Government Operations, *Financial Management in the Federal Government*, Senate Document No. 11 87th Congress, 1st Session (Washington: Government Printing Office, 1961), p. 133.

by Congress. We propose to demonstrate each year in our project activity schedule that we have executed our programs and expended the funds . . . in accordance with the intent of Congress."[70]

Although a description of the object for which the committee is appropriating is not legislation in an appropriations act, the performance budget substantially reduces the number of objects described. In essence, if Congress desires to keep the statute simple and meaningful, it must leave important areas of control to nonstatutory devices. Hence, the performance budget restricts the use of statutory specification of purpose—the technique that rarely runs afoul of points of order.

Congress has given up any ideas of controlling the executive through detailed appropriation acts. Consequently, nonstatutory money earmarks in the reports have vastly increased in frequency and importance. Prior to 1951 the Bureau of Mines budget contained specific itemization in the statute for programs in coal, petroleum, ferrous metals, and the like. The performance budget concept meant that all these activities were combined into a lump sum for "conservation and development of mineral resources." In 1954 the statute included $12,178,184 for mineral resources but did not allocate a specific amount for any particular program. Yet the House report stated that the following amounts had been allowed:

FUELS:

| | |
|---|---|
| *Coal* | $ 2,050,000 |
| *Petroleum and Natural Gas* | $ 1,343,356 |
| *Synthetic Liquid Fuels* | $ 1,267,000 |
| *Helium* | $ 90,795 |

MINERALS:

| | |
|---|---|
| *Ferrous metals and alloys* | $ 1,793,719 |
| *Nonferrous metals* | $ 3,585,125 |

70. House Hearings on Interior Appropriations for 1951 (85-1), Vol. I, p. 2.

| | | |
|---|---|---|
| *Nonmetallic minerals* | $ | 833,292 |
| *Mineral research, unclassified* | $ | 860,000 |
| *Control of fires in inactive coal deposits* | $ | 354,925 |

TOTAL                                    $12,178,814*

* House Report (83-314), p. 20.

Thus, nonstatutory techniques govern which minerals will be developed or conserved at a rapid rate. If Congress specified this in the statute, it would have contradicted the basic rationale for this performance budget.

The Tennessee Valley Authority budget provides another interesting example of the frequency and significance of non-statutory control caused by the performance budget. The TVA section of the 1956 appropriations statute reads: "For the purpose of carrying out the provisions of the Tennessee Valley Authority Act of 1953, as amended (16 U.S.C. Ch. 12A) including hire, maintenance, and operation of aircraft and purchase (not to exceed two hundred for replacement only) and hire of passenger motor vehicles, $14,903,850 to remain available until expended."[71]

The statute regulates only the total amount spent by TVA. Except for a proviso relating to the Dixon-Yates controversy, the 1956 act says nothing about how this $14 million should be apportioned among TVA's various activities. This is left to the report, which among other things:

1. states that TVA should proceed at once with two new generating units at the Fulton site to meet the impending shortage of power by 1958 (these units were not requested);

2. eliminates a contingency item for $100,000 and cuts $100,000 from the allotment for governmental relations and the economic staff;

3. criticizes the chairman of TVA because his statements before the committee "were confused and unconvincing";

71. Public Law 84-112.

4. specifies $100,000 for investigation of future projects;

5. because of private willingness to expand fertilizer production, "instructs" TVA to limit its fertilizer production to 5,000 tons;

6. specifies $1,000,000 for resource development;

7. and reduces requests for flood control operation and agronomic research.[72]

On the surface the earmarks in the report appear only slightly different from those in the statute, and thus, the changes made by the performance budget are more apparent than real. Does it matter whether the amount for coal research is in the statute or the report?

The most obvious difference is that nonstatutory money earmarks are not legally binding upon administrators. A State Department administrator who feels the national interest demands more money for diplomacy in Africa can disregard the committee report at his own peril. But the recent trend toward less detailed statutory control is more meaningful than this. Most important, the increase in nonstatutory controls enables administrators and legislators to transfer and adjust fund levels to meet the exigencies of rapidly changing conditions. Such transfers were precluded by the rigid statute.

The argument over whether Congress should legislate appropriations in detail began with Jefferson and Hamilton. Hamilton believed that detailed budget legislation would result in inadequate flexibility. He asserted administrators could not meet emergencies or adjust to outside circumstances if they were frozen into a predetermined expenditure pattern. However, the Jeffersonians triumphed over the Hamiltonians, as the appropriations acts specified everything from stationery to hay.

Wilmerding's research covering the period from 1784 to 1840 demonstrates that Congress was frequently frustrated in its attempts to appropriate in great detail.[73] In cases in which appropriations were overly rigid, the administration disre-

72. House Report (84-747), pp. 2-4.
73. Wilmerding, *Spending Power, passim.*

garded or evaded the statutory provisions, and Congress was often forced to sanction violations of the law. Some of the means employed to avoid statutory limitations included: confusing Congress by accounting procedures, drawing the teeth out of some requirements by legal interpretation, and pleading necessity.[74] In spite of such practices, there was a ready acquiescence on the part of individual congressmen or party factions who desired the illegal transfers of funds. Wilmerding concluded that detailed appropriations acts contain inherent limitations which, when exceeded, are self-defeating in practice. On the other hand, administrators who followed the statute lost all flexibility to meet contingencies because their appropriations were specified in such great detail.

Congress now realizes that while Congressional control by detailed statute sounds feasible in theory, experience shows that nonstatutory devices are more effective in practice— hence, the acceptance by Congress of Hoover Commission recommendations for a performance budget.

Since nonstatutory earmarks are not inflexible, administrators and legislators meet throughout the year to agree on transfers among report earmarks. For example, if Congress and the executive should agree that helium development must be intensified, funds could be transferred from coal development. Instead of evading a rigid statutory specification and hoping that no Congressional reaction will be forthcoming, administrators under a performance budget concept are able to negotiate with the subcommittee. In turn, nonstatutory control enables Congress to assume an active role in the continuous adjustment of funds for specific purposes, instead of being forced to sanction a *fait accompli* or take drastic action. The case against detailed statutory specification of purpose is presented by the late Secretary of State Dulles: "Our budget processes require that we prepare our estimates from 6 to 18 months in advance. . . . It is impossible for us to forecast accurately world developments to an

74. *Ibid., passim.*

extent that would permit us to pinpoint our precise needs. It is necessary . . . that we have reasonable flexibility in shifting funds."[75] He concluded: "This need was recognized several years ago when the Congress consolidated numerous general appropriations into one 'Salaries and Expenses' appropriation."[76]

The subcommittees prefer to be informed immediately about each proposed transfer, rather than permit the agency to make several transfers, and then review these transfers after considerable time has elapsed. The Interior Department requested transfer authority in fiscal 1962 for any "unforeseen or high priority requirements." The House committee denied the request and commented: "The committee has always been ready to consider specific problems judged by the Agency or Department involved to be outside their existing latitude."[77]

A STATISTICAL COMPARISON

The infrequent use of *new* statutory provisos that attach conditions to federal spending is indicative of the numerical preponderance of nonstatutory controls. Ordinarily in any one year, no more than five new provisos are included in an appropriations act.[78] By contrast in a committee report of thirty to forty pages there are normally thirty new nonstatutory controls that are not related to a monetary amount. It is particularly note worthy that a large majority of both the new and existing provisos involve minor housekeeping matters such as: transportation, transfer of funds between agencies or departments, number of employees in certain grades, state and local matching requirements, and uniforms.

75. Senate Hearings on State Department Appropriations for 1959 (85-1), p. 58.
76. *Ibid.*, p. 33.
77. House Report (87-233), p. 14.
78. The writer examined the new provisos in each of the Appropriations Acts included in the study (except Defense Department) for the years 1953-62.

Professor Holbert Carroll conducted an intensive survey of provisions included in the Mutual Security Appropriations Acts. His findings support the conclusion of this study based on the Public Works, Interior, Agriculture, Defense, Labor—Health, Education and Welfare, and State Department Acts.

> Scores of limitations inserted in the appropriations bills in the three areas studied did not materially affect the substance of policies or the administration of foreign affairs. A few were inserted at the request of the executive branch to take care of minor matters overlooked by the legislative committee. Most were designed to permit the committee to exercise more detailed fiscal control over aspects of administration. Regularly, for instance, the committee limited the number of employees that could be hired in certain grades and restricted the amount of money that would be used for new vehicles, for salaries in named ranks, for entertainment purposes, and the like.
> Many other limitations were of a borderline variety where it could be argued that the committee was trespassing into the realm of policy-making. A *few* clearcut examples of such excursions, especially through the device of legislative provisions, were uncovered in each of the areas studied.[79]

A statistical comparison of nonstatutory devices included in the reports and all types of statutory controls is presented in the following chart covering four selected years for four appropriations acts. The chart understates the number of extralegal devices because it excludes guidance in the hearings or in floor speeches.

79. Holbert N. Carroll, *House of Representatives and Foreign Affairs* (Pittsburgh: University of Pittsburgh Press, 1958), p. 167. Emphasis added. See also, Morgan Thomas, "Appropriations Control and the Atomic Energy Program," *Western Political Quarterly*, 9 (1956), 713-23. The AEC provisos are restricted to four areas: personnel, travel, construction, and community management.

*Why Employ Nonstatutory Techniques*

FREQUENCY CHART—STATUTORY AND NONSTATUTORY CONTROLS*

| APPROPRIATIONS | FISCAL | YEAR | | |
|---|---|---|---|---|
| AGRICULTURE | *1956* | *1959* | *1961* | *1963* |
| Statutory (House) | 45* | 47 | 50 | 48 |
| Nonstatutory (House) | 103** | 120 | 127 | 86 |
| INTERIOR | | | | |
| Statutory (Senate) | 47 | 61 | 72 | 69 |
| Nonstatutory (Senate) | 33 | 23 | 167 | 158 |
| LABOR—*HEW* | | | | |
| Statutory (House) | 86 | 84 | 103 | 110 |
| Nonstatutory (House) | 64 | 103 | 138 | 90 |
| PUBLIC WORKS | | | | |
| Statutory (House) | 20 | 35 | 32 | 30 |
| Nonstatutory (House) | 314 | 340 | 528 | 540 |

*Includes all appropriation accounts plus limitations and legislative provisions *not previously included* in the act. Limitations that are unchanged from year to year are not counted.
**Includes only nonstatutory devices that have not appeared in previous years.

Naturally, an explanation of the reason for a budget cut or increase was not computed as a nonstatutory device. Also, when a report comment clarified obscure statutory language, it was not considered a nonstatutory control. Only when the report pointed out which specific programs or objects were or were not affected by a cut or increase was it tabulated as an extralegal control. Indeed, if the administrator decided to observe the report, he would not absorb the cut in areas in which the report ratified the budget request.

Three of the acts—interior, agriculture, and public works—demonstrate an overwhelming majority of nonstatutory devices. For each of these acts, the number of nonstatutory strictures (as compared to statutory provisions) is either increasing substantially over the period covered or demonstrates a consistent numerical preponderance. The Labor—Health, Education and Welfare Act presents a fluctuating trend but the difference in frequency for the two types of controls is not substantial.

The primary causes for this preponderance of nonstatutory devices have been presented—the unique role and Congressional preference for nonstatutory controls. The frequency of extralegal devices is also influenced greatly by the appropriations structure of each bill, particularly the incidence of construction accounts. Under the performance budget as many as two hundred construction projects are combined in one appropriation. The report, however, earmarks budget amounts for each local project.

On the other hand, the number of statutory provisions is increased by the "unreformed" nature of some appropriations acts. For example, separate salary and expense accounts for each program are still prevalent for many of the agencies in the Labor–HEW act. These appropriation structure variables account for a substantial part of the frequency variance among the four bills. Consequently, a comparison between two different bills is meaningless.

SUMMARY

Some of the qualities of nonstatutory controls were summarized by Representative Sullivan (D.-Mo.) in 1962: "As usual, the report accompanying the [Labor–Health, Education and Welfare] bill prods, stimulates, encourages, directs, and scolds the agencies . . . to do a better job with the generous funds we give them and to use imagination and courage in pursuing new avenues of service to the public."[80]

The statute is employed to prescribe, forbid, and specify. The hearings and reports, either because they are not subject to a point of order or are the preferred technique, are used to rebuke, warn, prod, and issue affirmative directions.

80. 108 *Congressional Record* 4748 (1962).

# V. Dangers of Nonstatutory Oversight Techniques

While the "proper" role of the appropriations committee includes control of substantive policy, it does not include the responsibility of the legislative committee to propose new legislation and change existing authority.[1] Indeed, the use of nonstatutory devices to circumvent a point of order would not be such an objectionable practice if it were not so effective.[2] Administrators believe the appropriations committee "can hurt them more" than the legislative committee can and that the appropriations committee is more likely to resort to sanctions.

Nonstatutory language that changes existing legislative authority often does not go unnoticed by the legislative committee. On several occasions, legislative committee members have bitterly objected to such language.[3]

1. The other important method is a waiver of points of order by the Rules Committee. For a discussion of this method see James A. Robinson, *The House Rules Committee* (Indianapolis: Bobbs-Merrill Co., 1964).

2. The proper roles for the appropriations and legislative committees with respect to new legislation and modification of existing authority will be analyzed in the concluding chapter.

3. 99 *Congressional Record* 7354 (1953). In 1960 a strong protest against legislation in an appropriations act was made by Representative Cooley (D.-N.C.), chairman of the House Agriculture Committee. His outburst was caused by a statutory proviso that prohibited the CCC from reclassing cotton after the time of sale.

REP. COOLEY: When did you (the House Appropriations Committee) start writing the checks? You are supposed to carry out the intent and purpose of the legislative committee of the Congress.

. . . Since when did the Appropriations Committee arrogate to itself such mighty power as to say that Congress authorizes an act but we will cut it off, notwithstanding the views, the unanimous views of all the Committees on Agriculture. . . . Who

Several times, appropriations committees employed non-statutory directives to solve a problem long before the legislative committee had even considered new legislation. The following is an extremely graphic statement of the appropriations committee's attitude.

> REP. ANDERSEN [ranking member]: . . . Despite the fact that our function is primarily fiscal in nature, this subcommittee has through the years rendered service to Agriculture far beyond the mere approval of funds. I might add extemporaneously that this subcommittee for several years appropriated funds for the school-lunch program before the Congress of the United States would even authorize such a program.
>
> That program was carried on for those several years . . . simply because we brought it out of this particular subcommittee with no regular authorization.
>
> . . . This committee . . . conceived the idea of a sales manager for Commodity Credit long before anyone ever thought of writing such a position into basic law.
>
> We have seen the need for constructive legislation and we have acted to meet the need. I could point . . . [to] several instances in which we prompted the legislative Committee on Agriculture to do certain things for the good of agriculture.[4]

An interesting case that supports Representative Andersen's assertion is that of the Senate Appropriations Committee's objecting to a House appropriations report because it "expressed views and made recommendations on [cotton export] program policy and operations which the [Senate] committee feels may be within the jurisdiction of the Standing

---

is going to run the Department of Agriculture? The Subcommittee on appropriations or the legislative committees of this Congress, and the Members of Congress themselves? If we yield to this limitation, then we have our only forum thereafter in the star chamber sessions of the Committee on Appropriations. You cannot even get into that room without special permission. (106 *Congressional Record* 10039, L960)

4. House Hearings on Agriculture Appropriations for 1957 (84-2), Part 4, p. 1549.

Committee on Agriculture and Forestry."[5] In spite of this Senate protest, the conferees reported in favor of the appropriateness of the House report.

"The conferees have considered statements contained in the reports of the two committees, particularly comments relative to 'cotton and other export subsidy programs.' They are in full agreement that it is the responsibility of the Committee on Appropriations of the House and Senate to review activities of the Department of Agriculture under all existing laws for which appropriations are proposed by the executive branch or are considered by the Congress. In carrying out this responsibility, they recognize that it is within the jurisdiction of such committees to recommend approval or disapproval of appropriations and to make comments and recommendations with regard to such programs and activities."[6]

The legislative committees have found themselves lagging behind in many policy areas because nonstatutory controls allow the appropriations committees to move ahead despite inadequate legislative authority. Often the areas in which the appropriations committees have seized the initiative are those which have been neglected by the legislative committees. As Professor Carroll notes: "The [appropriations] committee reports on the support of American occupational policy in Europe and Asia contained the most words of advice. It will be noted shortly that the listless attitude of the legislative committee regarding occupation policy provided an opportunity for the Committee on appropriations to exercise unusually detailed control."[7]

To combat this practice, some legislative committee members are convinced that detailed prescriptions must be included in the authorizing legislation. If ample discretion is left to the administrator in the basic legislation, the appropriations committees will fill in the detailed requirements through nonstatutory language that circumvents the rules.

5. Senate Report (85-1438), p. 3.
6. House Report (85-1776), p. 6.
7. Holbert N. Carroll, *The House of Representatives and Foreign Affairs* (Pittsburgh: University of Pittsburgh Press, 1958), p. 165.

*Government without Passing Laws*

INTERNAL SUBCOMMITTEE PROCEDURE

Since the committee report is the most effective and important nonstatutory device, the procedure used to decide what language is included in an appropriations report is of critical importance. Generally, the report is largely the handiwork of the subcommittee chairman and the professional staff member assigned to the subcommittee.[8] As is the case for many areas of non-statutory control, their roles vary with personalities, customs, and circumstances. Since there is little in the printed record concerning the chairman's precise power in formulating report comments, interview data must be relied upon. Of particular interest is the question of whether the committee chairman's power is greater with respect to nonstatutory guidance than statutory requirements.

An initial hypothesis was that, while formal subcommittee votes are taken on most statutory language, the subcommittee chairman has a free hand in determining nonstatutory instructions. Though some executive officials agreed with this hypothesis, budget officers and committee staff, who have the best knowledge of the internal procedure of appropriations subcommittees, claim it is inaccurate (their view is substantiated by the writer's inspection of the subcommittee mark-up notes).[9]

The staff's role in formulating the committee report is necessarily heavy, for he must draw up the skeleton form of the report and the bill, called a "mark-up agenda," and, after the full subcommittee review, write the final draft. The staff's original suggestions for the mark-up agenda stem from several sources. During the hearings the chairman from time to time tells the staff to include in the report a subject under current discussion. In addition, the staff carefully checks the hearings transcript for issues he thinks the committee will want to discuss in its report. After a preliminary discussion

8. Since the full committee rarely alters the subcommittee's report draft, it is appropriate to refer to the Appropriations Committee report as a subcommittee report.

9. Executive officials such as an assistant secretary for administration agreed with the writer's initial hypothesis.

with the chairman, the staff prepares a rough draft of the mark-up agenda that includes both statutory and nonstatutory requirements. The staff then discusses the rough draft in great detail with the chairman. In many instances the chairman anticipates probable objections by other subcommittee members and adjusts nonstatutory and statutory language to meet such objections.

After the subcommittee chairman approves it, the mark-up agenda is mimeographed for distribution at the subcommittee meeting, and consequently the discussion does not start with a blank slate. It is significant that this mark-up agenda includes both statutory *and* nonstatutory proposals. In some subcommittees, the ranking member may have a part in formulating the mark-up agenda, but this role varies, depending largely on the importance of minority support in House and Senate conference committees.[10]

Some mark-up agendas have the statutory line amount for a particular agency and any proposed provisos on one page, and on the following page the proposed nonstatutory money earmarks and directives. Other committees prefer to have proposals for nonstatutory language next to the lump sum allowed in the statute for the agency or activity. The important point is that the full subcommittee reviews and discusses nonstatutory language in essentially the same manner as statutory. Thus, before they are included in the report nonstatutory controls are considered, or at least inspected superficially by all members of the subcommittee.

Normally, the subcommittees do not take formal votes on either statutory or nonstatutory language but rather reach consensus through discussion. If there are disagreements the members negotiate their differences until a compromise is reached. Once again note the procedure is identical for both types of control.

For unusually controversial nonstatutory directives, there may be protracted subcommittee negotiations on the specific

10. In some conference committees the minority member of the House or Senate Subcommittee is the "swing man" who can cast the deciding vote between two long-standing factions.

wording. Occasionally, subcommittee disputes over nonstatutory language appear in the printed record.

> Sen. Mundt: I invite attention to another paragraph . . . of the report. . . .
> "The committee has received complaints about the handling of storage in privately owned warehouses. The Department is requested to take the necessary steps to distribute these warehoused surplus commodities equitably among the grain producing states. . . ."
> As our Chairman recalls, I opposed that paragraph in our committee deliberations. I raised some questions about it, because to me it was not clear exactly what instructions we were delivering to the Department of Agriculture. My reason for opposing the paragraph was that it seemed to hint a little at an amendment called the Yates amendment, which came to us at one time from the House, and which we summarily rejected.[11]

If a member can gain enough subcommittee support for his protest, the chairman will strike out the nonstatutory language. However, as stated previously, the chairman frequently tries to anticipate possible objections and makes adjustments before the mark-up agenda is presented to the full subcommittee.

Not all nonstatutory controls are initiated by the staff in conjunction with the chairman. For example, in 1962 Representative Michel (R.-Ill.), the junior Republican member on the House Agriculture Subcommittee, proposed a nonstatutory directive.

> Rep. Michel: I wanted to amend this report, but it was ruled out by a three-vote margin in our [sub]committee, to require every [Agriculture Conservation Program] loan application in excess of $5 million to come before our committee so we could take a look and see what it is actually for.[12]

11. 108 *Congressional Record* 16501 (1962).
12. 108 *Congressional Record* 13615 (1962).

This example also illustrates the fact that for controversial nonstatutory directives a subcommittee vote may be required. While nonstatutory and statutory language is discussed *in general terms* during the subcommittee mark-up, the staff and the chairman draft the detailed and specific language that appears in the report. The mark-up agenda includes only an abbreviated form of the eventual report instruction. Thus, in many cases the chairman has the opportunity to decide which nonstatutory directives merit "mandate language." More important, at this stage the chairman can insert new directives that have not been cleared with the rest of the subcommittee. The frequency of this practice depends mainly on the attitude of the subcommittee chairman. In 1955, for example, two junior members of the House Agriculture Subcommittee complained that they had never seen many report statements "fraught with political implications and inaccuracies" until they arrived at the full committee meeting. The following floor colloquy ensued.

REP. HALLECK: The gentleman [Chairman Whitten] said, I believe, that "I wrote the report" and the gentleman now says "It is my report." Are we to understand from what the gentleman has said on two occasions in truth and in fact that this report is his personal report.

REP. WHITTEN: In so far as the wording of the report is concerned, it speaks for itself. In so far as the preparation of it is concerned, I helped put it together and submitted it to the members of my committee in line with what we ordinarily do here. And it was made available to all members of the subcommittee on Thursday prior to its being printed.

MR. VURSELL [R.-Ill., Junior Member of Subcommittee]: We were invited to the [full] committee . . . The gentleman [Chairman Whitten] was explaining the bill when I got in, about three minutes late. Of course it was more interesting to hear him explain the bill than it was to begin to read the committee reports, and that is the first time that I had seen it. . . . I was a little surprised as was my colleague from Washington [Mr. Horan] because I had hardly expected the criticism in the report that I found.

REP. ANDERSEN [ranking Republican member]: . . . [Chairman Whitten] did tell me that a copy of the report was available in our clerk's room to look over and scrutinize. That is the usual procedure in our subcommittee. I do feel sure that if the gentleman from Washington [Mr. Horan] *had asked* at the time to look at the report, [Chairman Whitten] certainly would have given him the same invitation.[13]

Representative Jensen, ranking member of the House Interior Subcommittee registered a similar complaint in 1955.

REP. JENSEN: I must say in all honesty that the matter was not discussed in [sub]committee to my knowledge. I did not know until I read the report, that the language he objects to was in the report. I had not an opportunity to read the report until it was laid before the full committee the very morning the full committee met. I cannot imagine how that language got in the report.[14]

A 1959 incident supports interview evidence that the wording of a report, and thus the decision on mandate language, is the chairman's responsibility. Representative Andersen, ranking member of the House Agriculture Subcommittee, disclosed on the floor that he disliked mandate language in a report directive dealing with the Agriculture Conservation Program. He continued: "As the gentleman well knows, the wording of any report is largely the wording of the chairman; and that is as it should be; but I want to say that when I read the report I had reservations with regard to the word 'fully'."[15]

Subcommittee members who disagree with the chairman's choice of words or instructions are able to protest in the full

13. 101 *Congressional Record* 3832-44 (1955). Emphasis added.
14. 101 *Congressional Record* 8333 (1955).
15. 105 *Congressional Record* 8316-17 (1959).

appropriations committee meeting. However, the full committee rarely changes a decision made by the subcommittee. In fact, in most instances the full committee can hardly be said to act at all. Professor Carroll's description of a full appropriations committee meeting on foreign aid funds could apply to almost any appropriations bill. "A morning meeting in July 1953 was typical. The subcommittee dealing with foreign aid appropriations had its bill read, reducing the President's request by more than a billion dollars. The bill, the report, and about four pounds of printed testimony, none of which committee members had seen before, were laid before the full committee. Within an hour, the committee had endorsed the subcommittee's recommendations without change. Four days later, the voice of the 10-man subcommittee had become the voice of the House."[16]

Before the full committee has considered a report, it has been distributed (without a number) bearing the notation that it is "subject to release when consideration of the bill has been completed by the whole committee."[17] Nonstatutory controls that are altered by the full committee normally deal with a highly controversial issue. For instance, report language that concerned the Dixon-Yates and Upper Colorado River disputes was debated and changed by the full committee after a formal vote.[18]

In the House Appropriations Committee, particularly, some mechanisms exist for committee-wide integration and control. Professor Richard Fenno demonstrates that the House committee is integrated by several norms which all members observe.[19] The House chairman, moreover, is able to appoint

16. Carroll, *House of Representatives and Foreign Affairs*, p. 146.
17. Arthur W. MacMahon, "Congressional Oversight of the Administration: The Power of the Purse," *Political Science Quarterly*, 58 (1943), 177.
18. See 107 *Congressional Record* 20995 (1961) with regard to Upper Colorado River. Also see 101 *Congressional Record* 9865 (1955), which documents that the full committee struck certain nonstatutory language pertaining to additional TVA steam units.
19. See Richard Fenno, *The Power of the Purse: Appropriations Politics in Congress* (Boston: Little, Brown and Co., 1966), *passim*.

subcommittee heads and rearrange subcommittee jurisdictions. He also sits as an ex-officio member along with the ranking member on all subcommittees. Yet the chairman seldom interferes with or supervises a subcommittee. This lack of supervision stems from several sources: a high regard for specialization shared by all members, the mutual deference that seniority commands, and the heavy work load of the chairman in the subcommittee he concentrates on.

CONCLUSION

The chairman of an appropriations subcommittee exercises tremendous influence over the content of both statutory and nonstatutory regulations. In two ways, however, the chairman's power is greater over nonstatutory controls, and consequently the danger of bias is enhanced.[20] The specific wording of a report is ordinarily entirely within the domain of the subcommittee chairman, and thus he can decide which directives merit mandate language. Moreover, when the chairman writes the report, he can add nonstatutory directives that are not subject to subcommittee review.[21]

It is evidently one thing for a chairman to add nonstatutory directives but quite another for him to change money earmarks in the bill or insert provisos without subcommittee

20. The subcommittee chairman answers most questions from the floor concerning nonstatutory controls. His answers can modify a nonstatutory directive, but sometimes other subcommittee members disagree with the chairman's views. As one legislator remarked:
> I have often thought that the chairman presumes what power he has in answering the questions addressed to him, in that he is speaking for the entire committee. I have disagreed with my chairman when he has said, "the committee feels so and so" in connection with an important point. Yet the only course is to rise and say, "I, for one, don't agree with my chairman in this interpretation," and only rarely will anyone get up and do that. That is the way legislative history is made in an interchange between the chairman and his questioner. (Charles L. Clapp, *The Congressman: His Work as He Sees It* [Washington: Brookings Institution, 1963, p. 136]

21. Sometimes the chairman informs the other members of the subcommittee just before floor consideration of additions he has made in the report.

clearance. Since the full committee rarely alters nonstatutory language, the subcommittee chairman can include a nonstatutory directive in the report without its being checked by anyone, unless the directive is the subject of a floor debate. Moreover, the subcommittee can ordinarily gain whole House approval of its proposals for nonstatutory directives.[22]

On balance, the differences in procedure for statutory and nonstatutory control are not substantial, and consequently the dangers of bias are only slightly higher for nonstatutory control.

INTERIM CHANGES IN NONSTATUTORY CONTROLS

It is customary for agencies to appeal some nonstatutory controls that they feel are unreasonable and thereby obtain subcommittee approval to disregard the report. This procedure is used most frequently for public works and water projects. By contrast, regulations that are included in the act cannot be modified or nullified by interim contact but must be amended by a law.

Ordinarily only the chairman and the ranking member of both subcommittees participate in such interim discussions.[23] More important, the rest of the subcommittee, the full committee, and the whole House have no opportunity to review decisions that often affect substantive policy and a considerable amount of federal funds. Since the law cannot be modified in this manner, the danger of bias inherent in such an informal review procedure is restricted to nonstatutory controls.

VOLUNTARY ORGANIZATIONS, INTERESTED INDIVIDUALS,
AND NONSTATUTORY CONTROLS

Near the end of the hearings, appropriations subcommittees hear testimony or accept written statements from interested

22. See Robert Wallace, *Congressional Control of Federal Spending* (Detroit: Wayne State University Press, 1960), p. 36, for why it is so difficult to amend appropriations bills.

23. All appropriations committee members and staff men interviewed agreed this was the case.

members, organizations, and individuals. The number of outside witnesses varies appreciably among the several committees. At one extreme is the House Corps of Engineers budget
hearings for 1956, which included 1,000 witnesses (other than
executive officials) who testified on behalf of local water projects. Only 126 outside witnesses testified during the 1959
House Hearings on Labor—Health, Education and Welfare
Appropriations. Most private individuals and organizations
support increased expenditures.

The implementation of the performance budget had important repercussions for interest groups. Congressional adoption of lump-sum appropriation titles meant that many interest group proposals for particular programs could no longer
be included in the act. In effect, the line item in the performance budget consolidated the favorite programs of many
voluntary organizations. Consequently, the language in the
committee report became the focus of interest group activity
and nonstatutory controls the prime method by which the
desires of various pressure groups were imposed upon the
executive.

Often a nonstatutory directive supported by an interest
group need only have the active support of one member for
committee approval. Although nonstatutory report directives are usually cleared informally with the entire subcommittee, proposed directives are likely to be objected to only
when a member is acquainted with the technicalities of the
interest-group proposal and feels strongly enough about it to
instigate a subcommittee battle. From the interest groups'
point of view, the easiest way to insure that nonstatutory language gets in the report is to persuade the chairman who for-
mulates the mark-up agenda.[24]

A reliable indicator that the committee is acting upon the

24. Interest-group proposals can also be transmitted by subcommittee members to the executive through informal interim techniques like
phone calls, letters, and meetings. An analysis of the proportion of
non-government witnesses appearing before the twelve appropriations
subcommittees is included in Fenno, *The Power of the Purse*, pp.
341-44.

advice of a pressure group is a report phrase such as, "It has come to the attention of the committee," or "the committee has the distinct impression."[25] For instance, in 1960 witnesses for the Oyster Institute and for the State Sanitary Engineers presented the House Labor—Health, Education and Welfare Subcommittee with figures concerning the infrequent inspection of milk, shellfish, and general sanitation in interstate commerce. The 1960 report revealed: "The committee has gained the distinct feeling that activities concerned with milk and food sanitation have been overshadowed by the larger program of air pollution and water pollution. . . . The Committee expects, within the amounts provided, additional amounts be given to the division's activities in connection with interstate shipment of milk, shellfish, sanitation. . . ."[26]

An interest group cannot effectively influence a program that is scattered among several divisions and budget allocations. In such circumstances outside witnesses will often urge an appropriations subcommittee to consolidate a program in one organizational unit with a single budget allocation. The 1961 Labor—Health, Education and Welfare report commented that the "committee will expect the 1962 budget to have environmental health activities consolidated in the Bureau of States Services." During hearings Chairman Fogarty admitted this directive had been instigated by private organizations. "This [consolidation] has been proposed by the voluntary groups. . . . They would like to see some of these [environmental health] activities set out by themselves."[27]

There is a danger that a few highly respected outside witnesses may serve as the impetus for a considerable amount of nonstatutory control, and thereby exercise an inordinate influence over agency policy and development. The National Institutes of Health provide a classic example.

25. These phrases may also be used if the committee is acting upon the advice of a fellow legislator.

26. House Report (86-309), p. 10.

27. House Hearings on Labor—Health, Education and Welfare Appropriations for 1961 (86-2), p. 34.

Each institute contains a national advisory council of non-government scientists chaired by the surgeon general. These advisory councils take formal action on applications for grants and research support. The doctors on the national advisory councils are intimately involved in the administrative details of the institutes because their grant decisions are based on such criteria as Public Health Service and Department of Health, Education and Welfare research and training policy, the significance of various research and training proposals, and the efficient expenditure of funds.

From 1950 to 1960 many of the most renowned members of the advisory councils appeared before the Labor—Health, Education and Welfare Appropriations Subcommittees and, in effect, were not just advisors but directors of the large and rapid expansion of NIH. In this period when total NIH appropriations increased from $52 million to nearly a billion dollars, the Eisenhower budget requests were never appreciably greater than the funds appropriated in the preceding year. Thus, with little technical advice from the executive branch, the subcommittees were forced to rely on the advice of doctors from the national advisory councils.

These outside experts not only decided program emphasis, but also determined qualitative changes as the various programs increased their scale by multiples. For a number of reasons, the subcommittees employed nonstatutory techniques to implement the recommendations of the advisory council doctors. The prime reasons were that many of the new programs required administrative flexibility and/or may have been subject to a point of order.

In 1959 Doctors Stare and Farber of Harvard and Debakey of Baylor testified that the National Institutes of Health's future growth required a number of centralized facilities to amalgamate research. Their recommendations included: (1) decentralization of research grant administration, (2) regional services like primate colonies and instrument centers, and (3) specialized clinical research facilities that could serve several scientists in a particular area.[28] The doctors' testimony outlined these facilities in vague terms, and made some rough estimates of the cost. Neither the House nor Senate subcommittee questioned them. " 'I happened to have lunch with Dr. Farber . . . the other day,—' Congressman Fogarty reveals, 'and I learned there is considerable sentiment for these (clinical research) centers.' Congressman Cederberg did not know of 'anyone who would in any way hamper these programs, because I had lunch with Dr. Farber. . . .' "[29]

In its report of 1959 the Senate Subcommittee recommended the precise amounts and facilities the doctors had urged and directed NIH to "proceed without delay."[30] However, NIH was not prepared to implement these requests because only preliminary studies of the various recommended programs and facilities had been completed.[31] In effect, the appropriations subcommittees, acting upon the advice of outside witnesses, were pushing NIH forward at a faster pace than the institutes were prepared for. By 1961 not one of the facilities recommended by the three doctors had been constructed. As an NIH administrator related, "We tried to put the brakes on this research facilities program, but the advisory groups complained directly to the Appropriations Subcommittees."

Obviously, these advisory councils provided Congress with a unique channel for monitoring NIH implementation of nonstatutory directives. It was no coincidence that Dr. Farber and Dr. Debakey were members of the *ad hoc* committee that selected sites for the same clinical research facilities these

28. See Senate Hearings on Labor—Health, Education and Welfare Appropriations for 1960 (86-1), testimony of Drs. Farber, Stare, and Debakey in Vol. III. Any attempt to implement these recommendations by legislation could be thwarted by a point of order challenging that the facilities added to existing law. An NIH administrator assured the writer that the clinical research centers proposed by the doctors were not authorized.

29. Aaron B. Wildavsky, *The Politics of the Budgetary Process* (Boston: Little, Brown and Co., 1964), p. 71.

30. Senate Report (86-425), pp. 23-24.

31. Information relative to this case was disclosed during interviews with NIH administrators.

two researchers had urged the subcommittees to initiate. After some subcommittee prodding, construction of the research centers was speeded up.[32]

There is considerable evidence that the NIH advisory councils are not unique. The Agriculture Research Service has numerous advisory councils that testify before the committees on appropriations. The statute carries a lump sum for all types of agricultural research, but the report earmarks and directs certain studies. Hence, many advisory council recommendations are included in the appropriations reports. In its 1957 report, however, the House Agriculture Subcommittee criticized the performance of these advisory councils:

> The Committee has felt that such a system of advisory councils would help to keep the research program of the Department on a sound and practical basis and has relied on such groups to provide the principal review of many individual projects proposed in the budget year. Instead of making a thorough and continuing review of existing research projects which might be improved or eliminated . . . the large increases proposed each year indicate that the time of these Committees is taken up largely with review and approval of new projects of special interest. . . .[33]

In summary, the performance budget limits the ability of interest groups to influence the language in an appropriations act. Nonstatutory devices, however, provide a compensating opportunity without going through the requirements of legal enactment. Since interest group demands in a representative

32. It was incidents of this type which led to the following exchange in the 1961 Labor–HEW hearings:

REP. LAIRD: We are getting to a position where the National Institutes of Health are really the responsibility of Congress. . . . Do you understand what I mean?

DR. TERRY [Assistant Director of Heart Institutes]: I certainly do.

REP. LAIRD: The National Institutes of Health could be compared to the General Accounting Office and the Library of Congress. It is becoming an Arm of Congress rather than a part of the Public Health Service. (House Hearings for 1962, p. 56)

33. House Report (85-438), p. 12.

system of government should be considered, this use of non-statutory controls is not necessarily undesirable. Furthermore, voluntary organizations and interested citizens provide the appropriations subcommittee with valuable information to supplement the testimony of the executive agencies.

Nevertheless, nonstatutory techniques enable groups or individuals with fragmented views of the public interest and the budgetary process to implement their conception of public policy. Whether nonstatutory devices encourage undesirable appropriations control depends on how carefully the subcommittees analyze pressure group requests.

PRESIDENTIAL CONTROL OF THE BUDGET

Often an agency is not permitted to implement certain programs or policies because of over-all budget ceilings or general departmental regulations. An agency is able to appeal its case directly or, more commonly, indirectly to an appropriations subcommittee. For a number of reasons, nonstatutory controls and informal meetings are uniquely suited in circumstances where an appropriations subcommittee and an agency want to impair the effectiveness of central executive machinery.[34] The result enhances what Professor Ernest Griffith calls "government by whirlpools of special interests and problems."[35]

Agency-subcommittee co-operation on nonstatutory controls is best illustrated by a process called the "mousetrap." If departmental or Budget Bureau regulations forbid a course of action, an agency attempts a mousetrap by soliciting a comment in the committee report endorsing the desired policy and attaching it to congressional intent. For example, nonmatching research facilities may be contrary to departmental

34. The writer believes there are some positive effects of executive disunity such as more flexibility for new program development, greater motivation for program leaders, and perhaps enhanced responsiveness to program needs in particular areas.

35. Ernest Griffith, *Congress: Its Contemporary Role* (New York: New York University Press, 1961), pp. 50-52. The subcommittees can more effectively control a bureau that is largely independent from central executive direction.

regulations. Nevertheless, the research agency will ask the departmental legal counsel for an opinion on what the appropriations report must say to sanction non-matching grants. A sympathetic appropriations subcommittee will subsequently insert the required phrase in its report.

A successful "mousetrap" often requires the use of non-statutory devices because it involves an affirmative direction subject to a point of order. The following exchange illustrates a National Institutes of Health "mousetrap" of the General Accounting Office's ruling against using research grants for renovation of laboratory facilities.

> DR. SHANNON [Director of NIH]: . . . we felt we were well within our authority and were well within the intent of Congress to use research grants as we have in the past for essential renovation.
>
> They [GAO] raised such a serious objection that they will not be satisfied by anything short of a statement by the appropriations committee concerned. Such a statement should indicate that it is the intent of the appropriating bodies that such a proportion of our grant funds as are essential for the achievement of and objects of project grants can be made available for renovation.[36]

Naturally, most "mousetraps" involve off-the-record contact that never appears in the hearings.

Some agencies and departments have had representatives present during subcommittee deliberations on a report. While this is rare, it deserves attention because the report is the most effective and frequently used nonstatutory technique. As Professor Arthur MacMahon observed:

> Under these circumstances, naturally, the report is likely to contain remarks that later will provide fulcrums whereby the department can exercise leverage upon its self-assertive parts. Such a nexus of departmental leaders and committee clerks is more than in-

36. House Hearings on Labor—Health, Education and Welfare Appropriations for 1962 (87-1), p. 425.

teresting. It is highly significant, for it illustrates two things: first, that the disciplinary strains in government are not a simple alignment of administration as a whole against legislative body; second, that pressure of the legislative body may be exerted in fortifying the central machinery within the administration itself. But reciprocal centripetalism is not simple; organs of supervision like the Bureau of the Budget must be considered. Sometimes legislative pressure may strengthen the independent position of favored agencies.[37]

With one exception, the administrators interviewed for this study disclosed that they never participated in subcommittee deliberations or the drafting of a report, while they do stay close to the phone or in the Capitol near the subcommittee's meeting room. Their only function is to offer technical advice upon request rather than negotiate or make suggestions. This practice is not likely to impede executive unity.

In many cases the Bureau of the Budget is a mutual antagonist of an agency and an appropriations subcommittee, and, therefore, both stand to gain if the Bureau's powers are weakened. The one cardinal rule administrators must follow is that the witness must never initiate or volunteer information that contradicts the President's budget. As one agency official remarked, "They have to worm it out of you. You're supposed to wait a decent length of time before you let your arm be twisted."[38]

In 1959 the Budget Bureau, despite objections by the appropriations committee, prevented the Labor Department from using an emergency fund for unemployment compensation. This interesting exchange took place in the 1959 hearings.

SEN. HILL: Mr. Secretary, I would like to go into this unemployment insurance.

As you know, we had quite a bit of discussion over

37. MacMahon, "Congressional Oversight," Vol. 58, p. 389.
38. See Fenno, *The Power of the Purse*, p. 303.

this in the last session and there has been quite a disagreement between the House and Senate about it.

MR. DODSON [Assistant Secretary of Labor]: I think
this is an administrative operating problem. We had
some problems with the Bureau of the Budget in getting the contingency fund released. . . .

SEN. HILL: To be frank, what I had in mind was
putting more authority in your hands and less in the
Bureau of the Budget's hands.

Now you think about that, Mr. Secretary, and inform us if you have any further thought or suggestion. . . .

MR. DODSON: May we go off the record for a moment, Mr. Chairman?[39]

Interim contact was probably used to work out some arrange-
ment that lessens the Bureau of the Budget's powers in this
area.

A thorough investigation of interim meetings and informal relationships is needed to ascertain the extent to which
nonstatutory techniques aid executive disunity. A device like
the "mousetrap" can be demonstrated, but only extensive interviews could reveal whether it is employed on a large scale.
Nevertheless, the point remains that nonstatutory techniques
provide an effective means whereby agencies and appropriations subcommittees can co-operate at the expense of administrative integration.

REVIEW BY THE ENTIRE HOUSE

The focus in the previous sections has been on abuses of nonstatutory devices. Briefly, these abuses include the use of
nonstatutory controls: to encroach upon the prerogative of the
legislative committee, to increase executive disunity, to impose the demands of pressure groups on the executive, and
to implement the biases of a subcommittee chairman without consideration by the rest of the subcommittee. Moreover,

39. See House Hearings on Labor–Health, Education and Welfare
Appropriations for 1962 (87-1), *passim*.

such abuses of nonstatutory techniques are seldom reviewed by the full appropriations committee that ordinarily ratifies a subcommittee's decisions in toto. As Arthur MacMahon observed: "It is not Congress, not the House or Senate, not even the appropriations committee as a whole that should be thought of as an abstraction set against the administration. The reality is a handful of men from particular states and districts, working with a particular committee clerk on a multitude of details."[40]

While MacMahon's assertion has substantial validity, it is erroneous to conclude that a handful of men on an appropriations subcommittee is not subject to some review and control by the entire legislative body. Obviously, statutory requirements in the committee bill can be stricken or amended on the floor. Numerous provisos and cuts have been initiated by floor action, and sometimes subcommittee bills with full committee endorsement are completely changed by floor amendments. But what about language in committee reports? Are abuses of nonstatutory controls reversed by the whole House?

At first glance it would appear that the subcommittees can operate unchecked with respect to nonstatutory regulation. It is impossible to amend language in a report since it is not legislation in a formal sense. The floor debate on an appropriations bill is frequently limited to two hours, and this seems barely sufficient for decisions on broad statutory expenditures. Further, many report directives are concerned with technical administrative problems that the ordinary member finds uninteresting and incomprehensible. If the entire House review is inadequate or nonexistent, the dangers of nonstatutory control become even more significant.

The writer examined all House and Senate floor debates from 1953 to 1962 on the appropriations bills included in this study. This examination revealed that to a substantial extent the whole House does review and modify nonstatutory controls recommended by the appropriations committees. In

40. MacMahon, "Congressional Oversight," Vol. 58, p. 181.

fact, there are five sources of protest against nonstatutory directives. These protest centers insure that this important type of appropriations control does not operate unchecked. If nonstatutory language is related to the responsibilities and interests of any one of these protest centers, it most likely will be monitored and, if found objectionable, may be modified on the floor.

The most obvious source of protest is from members who believe nonstatutory language will have an adverse impact on their constituents. Many constituents and interest groups examine report language and, if they object, contact their representatives in Congress. In 1962 Senator Mundt of South Dakota strongly objected to a directive in the agriculture report: "I have received a great many inquiries . . . from farmers who raise and store grain on their farms, and from operators of elevators."[41]

State and local governments provide another source of constituency protest against nonstatutory regulations. Since nonstatutory devices are not subject to points of order, the appropriations committees are able to alter policy aspects of federal-state or federal-local matching programs. In 1962 Senator Pell (D.-R.I.), at the request of the Rhode Island Unemployment Compensation Bureau, tried to modify a Senate report comment that recommended consolidation of the local unemployment compensation and employment services.[42] Any provisions to this effect in the appropriations bill could have been successfully challenged as legislation in an appropriations act.

The second protest center includes congressmen who, for some reason other than the interests of their constituency, are enthusiastic and deeply concerned about the development of a particular program. A member who sponsors legislation establishing a program will frequently oppose nonstatutory controls that retard or alter its development. Senator Fulbright played a key role in the successful initiation of a

41. 108 *Congressional Record* 16501 (1962).
42. 108 *Congressional Record* 12293 (1962) and 108 *Congressional Record* 13120 (1962).

program for international educational exchange. Accordingly, Senator Fulbright protects international exchanges from nonstatutory regulations he feels are unwise.

For example, in 1956 the Senate report alleged there had been a lack of association by United States exchange students with local people and that our students were too heavily concentrated in a few universities.[43] Senator Fulbright proceeded to rebut each criticism the Senate Appropriations Committee made. "I do not know where the committee got these impressions; and if they were true, I too, would deplore such a situation. However, as you know, I have been very much interested in this program, have kept in touch with its operation, and I must say I think the picture painted by the committee in its report is decidedly exaggerated."[44]

There are many members of Congress who have a particular interest in certain programs. Representative Bolton (R.-Ohio), a member of the Foreign Service Institute Board, resisted nonstatutory directives he felt might hinder effective operation of the institute.[45] Representative Sullivan (D.-Mo.) commented adversely on several nonstatutory instructions relating to the Food and Drug Administration.[46] Nonstatutory guidance with an appreciable impact on agencies or programs within the jurisdiction of a legislative committee will often be reviewed by members of the legislative committee.[47] For example, the Joint Committee on Atomic Energy tries to counteract nonstatutory controls that it believes might have a detrimental effect on the atomic energy program.

The third protest center is the result of the legislative committees' resisting infringements by the appropriations committees on their prerogative. Usually the counsel and/or some members of a substantive committee will examine the appro-

43. 102 *Congressional Record* 8997 (1956).
44. *Ibid.*, 8997.
45. 106 *Congressional Record* 7391 (1960).
46. 107 *Congressional Record* 8247 ff. (1961).
47. Unlike the third protest center that is concerned with appropriations encroachment upon the legislative committee's prerogative, this protest center is caused by the legislative committee's disagreement with the appropriations committee's recommendations.

priations report, and thus will be aware of nonstatutory language calculated to circumvent a point of order. In 1947 Clifford Hope (R.-Kan.), former chairman of the House Agriculture Committee, set forth the legislative committee's view by stating that to allow legislation to be written by the appropriations committee would set it up as "a great super committee which will undermine the authority, activity, and importance of all legislative committees."[48]

Language in an appropriations report which is regarded by one party as a partisan political blast ordinarily provokes the fourth protest center. The 1955 House Agriculture report contained wide-ranging criticism of the policies of Republican Secretary of Agriculture Benson. The criticism was authored without subcommittee clearance by Jamie Whitten, the Democratic chairman of the House Agriculture Subcommittee. House Republicans strongly objected to the partisan tone of criticism like the following:

> There is much to indicate that with the Department of Agriculture, a branch of the Executive Department, political and other considerations predominate to the point of preventing action. Proper actions by the [Commodity Credit] Corporation are made subservient to a host of other considerations, many of which, in the opinion of a majority of the committee, are unsound. These actions of the Secretary of Agriculture and others about him are hard to understand, unless CCC costs and losses are for use to support their determined efforts to change the price support program[49]

The Republicans did not allow this political attack to go unchallenged but rather asserted that the report was "fraught with political implications and inaccuracies."[50] Several speakers including Minority Leader Halleck (R.-Ind.) contended the report did not express the views of the House of Representatives but only of certain Democrats.

48. 3 *Congressional Quarterly* 211 (1947).
49. House Report (84-303), p. 6.
50. 101 *Congressional Record* 3832 (1955).

A subcommittee split over nonstatutory language may result in some form of floor protest against the committee report. Minority reports on appropriations bills are rare because of the committee norm of unity. Professor Richard Fenno discovered that 95 per cent of all appropriations bills in the period 1947-57 were reported by the committee without dissent.[51] However, a floor protest by a subcommittee member concerning nonstatutory language is not likely to impair subcommittee unity to the same extent as a minority report. In fact, in many instances subcommittee members disagree with the wording of nonstatutory directives. For example, Representative Andersen of the House Agriculture Subcommittee claimed he preferred the phrase "cooperate as far as possible" in place of the 1959 Agriculture report language of "fully cooperate."[52]

Since the five protest centers cover a wide spectrum of interests and viewpoints, nonstatutory language frequently involves at least one of them: a constituent, a program some member is particularly interested in, the legislative committee's jurisdiction, partisan politics, or a split within an appropriations subcommittee. If nonstatutory language is objectionable to any of these sources of protest, modification or even nullification may be attempted during the floor debate.

Departments and agencies are aware of the five protest centers, and thus know where they can get assistance to alter nonstatutory controls. It is a standard maneuver for an administrator to contact members of Congress who are sympathetic to an agency or departmental viewpoint on a nonstatutory directive. Furthermore, agencies often write speeches for Congressional use in opposing nonstatutory language.

On several occasions members of Congress have stated on the floor that the executive branch urged them to protest against nonstatutory instructions. In 1954 Representative Smith (D.-N.J.) opposed a report directive abolishing the

51. See Richard Fenno, "House Appropriations Committee as a Political System," *American Political Science Review* 56 (1962), 316-17.
52. 105 *Congressional Record* 8316 (1959).

State Department's Metals and Minerals Staff. "Therefore, the State Department has requested me to make this statement for the *Record*, so that the matter can be considered at the time of the conference."[53] Representative Roosevelt (D.-Cal.) contended during a 1958 floor debate that several House report directives on foreign language training were unwise, "In view of the fact that I was informed just today by someone from the Department of State that the gentleman from New York [Chairman Rooney] was sabotaging foreign language training."[54]

In short, the departments and bureaus keep their friends on the Hill informed about nonstatutory controls of mutual concern.[55] Thus, the administration and the five protest centers interact to insure that many nonstatutory directives are considered by the whole House.

There are three methods by which non-members can modify or nullify nonstatutory controls initiated by the appropriations committees. Since it is not legislation, there is no way that language in a committee report can be formally amended. However, an amendment can be so phrased as to specifically offset a nonstatutory instruction in a report. This method has been successful in several instances.

In 1953 the House Interior Department report instructed the department to dispose of three synthetic fuel demonstration plants. Several representatives from districts involved protested the directive and managed to enlist several allies who objected to turning over the government plants to private industry. The opposition became so strong that Representative Fenton, the floor manager, decided to accept an amendment that provided funds for continued operation of the demonstration plants.[56] In a similar case, Representative Budge (R.-Idaho) gained entire House acceptance of an amendment nullifying report language which deleted Idaho

53. 100 *Congressional Record* 8136 (1954).
54. 104 *Congressional Record* 8883 (1958).
55. This point was stressed during interviews.
56. 99 *Congressional Record* 4140 (1953).

from the Bureau of Reclamations 1955 general investigation program.

> REP. BUDGE: Mr. Chairman, I have discussed the language which I am submitting, with the Members of the western panel who wrote the language in the report which my language is intended to correct. The language here is simply intended to clarify the language which is contained in the report; and so far as I know, there is no objection to it.[57]

But examples of amending the appropriations bill to counteract nonstatutory directives are rare, for, as we have stressed previously, it is extremely difficult to amend an appropriations bill.

A 1956 speech by State Department Subcommittee Chairman Rooney reflects the confidence of the appropriations committee with respect to amendments. In effect, Rooney dares Representative Judd to try to amend the bill and Judd refuses.

> REP. JUDD: But in any case I protest this method of legislation. If the committee had put language in the bill . . . then we could offer an amendment to strike out the provision.
>
> REP. ROONEY: But all the gentleman needs to do, if he thinks we should spend $9 a head to show Cinerama to the Cambodians on this flat-top, is to offer an amendment providing the amount deleted in the report. That will put it right before the House for its decision one way or another.
>
> REP. JUDD: . . . Mr. Chairman, because this proposal has real merit . . . I want to describe it here and express the hope the Senate committee will consider it more favorably.[58]

Unlike most other committees, moreover, the appropriations committee can be practically certain its bill will not be defeated on the floor. Since a few dissatisfied legislators are

57. 101 *Congressional Record* 8496 (1955).
58. 102 *Congressional Record* 7007 (1956).

not able to jeopardize the bill's chances of passage, the committee is not likely to accept amendments designed to offset report comments.

Since amendments to an appropriations bill are ordinarily unsuccessful, nonstatutory directives are usually modified through floor colloquies. Such colloquies may aim at persuading the appropriations committee to "amend" nonstatutory language by making supplemental legislative history. A floor colloquy can elicit a statement from a subcommittee chairman that a certain nonstatutory directive is not intended to be a mandate but merely a suggestion. Hence, congressmen who oppose a report directive have put the administrator in a position where he can disregard or compromise the committee's desires without risking some negative committee action.

A controversial 1958 agriculture report statement combining meat and poultry inspection provides a good example of this type of modification of committee report language.

> REP. DIXON [R.-Utah]: The gentleman [Chairman Whitten] made a statement wondering whether the Department would carry out the suggestion of the committee. . . .
>
> REP. WHITTEN [Subcommittee Chairman]: May I say that the Department has the broad authority and we have indicated to them that if, in the exercise of their direction they prevent this needless duplication, they will not be breaking faith with the committee. That is all that is involved here.
>
> Whether it is utilized or not, the authority exists.
>
> REP. LANDRUM [D.-Ga.]: . . . I believe the statements [of Mr. Whitten], together with the legislative history of the Poultry Products Inspection Act is sufficient advice to the Secretary of Agriculture as to the Congressional intent . . . and I trust there will be no consolidation.[59]

59. 104 *Congressional Record* 5975 (1958). Note the opposition came from the legislative committee, which objected to the infringement upon their jurisdiction.

The effect of the floor colloquy was to give the Agriculture Department more discretion.

Several members of the Senate managed to establish additional legislative history, with respect to a 1953 report criticism of "split project" hospital construction under the federal-state matching program. A "split project" enables a state to grant to applicants only part of the money required for construction, and consequently, the appropriations committees must appropriate the remainder or else suspend construction of a partially built hospital. In order to extend the use of split projects, Senator Humphrey asked Chairman Thye (R.-Minn.) if it were not true that the committee report implied a "yellow light" rather than a "red light" on split projects. When Thye replied in the affirmative, Humphrey said he wanted the record perfectly clear so that the executive could not point to the report and forbid future split projects.[60]

Sometimes the appropriations committee refuses to allow floor debates to modify extralegal controls and committee considers mandatory. The 1956 Senate Labor–Health, Education and Welfare report directed the Labor Department to furnish the Senate Appropriations Committee with a list of all visits by Labor Department officials to members of Congress along with the type of business discussed. Senator Saltonstall (R.-Mass.) tried to give the Labor Department enough leeway to ignore the directive:

> SEN. SALTONSTALL: So that in the opinion of the distinguished chairman of the subcommittee, it would *not be compulsory* on the part of the Department of Labor, but the information would be helpful for the Congress to have?
>
> SEN. HILL: I would say that when Congress requests certain information from a department . . . it becomes the *obligation* and the *duty* of the department to supply the information.[61]

60. 99 *Congressional Record* 10072 (1953).
61. 101 *Congressional Record* 7617 (1955). Emphasis added.

Apart from modifying the obligatory nature of a nonstatutory directive, dissatisfied members may seek a revision of the substance of such a directive through floor exchanges. Senator Fulbright, for example, changed the emphasis of a 1960 directive which specified that educational exchanges with West Europe should be "sharply reduced." After a strong protest, Fulbright received assurances from Senator Ellender that the reduction applied only to the money above the current appropriations and did not imply a reduction in the existing program.[62]

Floor colloquies are employed to exempt particular cases or situations from a general prohibition advanced in the committee report. The 1958 Agriculture report instructed the Commodity Credit Corporation to hold formal hearings with recorded testimony before it undertook any "major action or change of policy." In order to mitigate the impact of this requirement, Representative Andersen requested a definition of what Chairman Whitten considered "major actions." "May I ask [Chairman Whitten] this question: Just what would the gentleman consider to be a major change in policy or a major action requiring formal hearings. . . . Will the gentleman kindly place in the *Record* at his convenience today any further definitions he might have relative to my question?"[63]

At the suggestion of the Agriculture Department, Senator Humphrey attempted to limit the applicable area of the following directive: "The [Agriculture] committee believes that in some areas of the country the travel, per diem, and related expenses for county offices and the use of county committeemen have been excessive. . . . Their [county committeemen] use in visiting individual farms and in the administration of county office programs should not be continued."[64] Senator Humphrey argued that special conditions in northern farm regions required travel and visits by elected county committeemen and Chairman Russell agreed to soften the directive.

62. 99 *Congressional Record* 10072 (1953).
63. 104 *Congressional Record* 5991 (1958).
64. 108 *Congressional Record* 16509 (1962).

"That [report] should have said 'probably' or 'unnecessarily.' We realize that there must be some visits to the individual farms to check on complaints."[65] Thus, supplemental legislative history changed the committee's intent from a prohibition of all visits to a warning against unnecessary visits.

If the appropriations committee is able to defeat amendments and is unwilling to alter nonstatutory language through a floor colloquy, there is a remaining course of action left for opponents. Floor speeches by one or several members can establish a contrary legislative history that furnishes some support for an administrator who disregards the committee's instructions.[66] This method does not involve colloquies with members of the appropriations committee but merely requires unilateral statements. Administrators are able to claim, with some justification, that a contrary floor record renders the committee report nonbinding. Further, the offsetting legislative history enables administrators to assert that they are not sure what the intent of Congress is, and therefore are justified in choosing the interpretation they prefer. Hence, executives sometimes try to persuade sympathetic members to make floor speeches stressing that there is deep disagreement within the chamber over certain nonstatutory language.

This strategy is most likely to succeed when several members voice their opposition to the committee's nonstatutory

65. *Ibid.* 16509.

66. Entire House review is also exercised over nonstatutory rebukes for unsatisfactory agency performances. Sympathetic members will defend an agency against what they believe is unjustified appropriations criticism even though the committee does not specify any policy changes. Chairman Rooney of the State Department committee in 1956 launched a general indictment of the State Department administration because an orchestra sent abroad under this cultural exchange program contained some Communists or near-Communists. Representative Coudert (R.-N.Y.) thought this orchestra incident did not merit a general indictment of State Department performance. "The fact is that the gentleman (Rooney) made something of a mountain out of a molehill in dealing with this matter. If one had not listened to him with the greatest of care one would have thought that these oboe players and trombone players were the ones who set policy in high places of government." 102 (*Congressional Record* 6983, 1956)

recommendations.[67]  For example, large-scale battle on the floor was triggered by a 1953 Interior Department Conference report statement that terminated the Southwest Power Administration's (SWPA) generating and transmission contracts with several electric power co-operatives.  Many powerful and respected members of both Houses strongly protested this action, and thus the SWPA asked the General Accounting Office for its opinion on the correct interpretation of the legislative history.  On the basis of the objections voiced on the floor, the GAO ruled the House did not accept the statements in the conference report with respect to the SWPA.

> . . . While the statement of the managers of the House accompanied the conference report and the conference report was agreed to by both Houses, there is nothing in the legislative history to indicate that the Congress approved or adopted the statement by the House managers.  In fact, such history discloses that some members of House and Senate questioned the effect of the House manager's statement.  In this connection, note the following statements made on the floor of the House and Senate during the debate on the conference report. . . .
>
> "MR. MONRONEY: The contingencies involved are before the Senate only because they are written in the House report, not in the bill itself, which, of course, as the statutory law will control.
>
> "MR. RAYBURN: We would like the language of the bill to be the law and not some statement by a bunch of conferees. . . ."
>
> It appears from the quoted statements that some members of the House and Senate did not consider the statement of the House managers as binding on the Congress.  Thus it is doubtful whether the agreement to the conference report indicates the Congress agreed with the statement of the House managers or whether

67. Some agencies said they point out to the appropriations committees specific speeches that support their position. Others said this procedure is useless, because the committee already knows about the motives behind such speeches.

it considered the statement not to be a part of the law and ineffective.[68]

Whether floor speeches can effectively counterbalance nonstatutory language depends in the main on the number and stature of the members who speak in protest. The SWPA case provoked opposition from such powerful and influential legislators as Representative Rayburn (D.-Tex.), Senator Symington (D.-Mo.), Senator Kerr (D.-Okla), Representative Anderson (R.-Minn.), and Senator Monroney (D.-Okla). The administration's grounds for disregarding the appropriations committee are not nearly as strong when only one or two members of Congress dispute a nonstatutory directive. For instance, in 1957 the Interior Department Conference report stipulated that the department should dispose of an oil shale conversion plant in Rifle, Colorado. Representative Vinson (D.-Ga.), chairman of the Armed Services Committee, objected because the Navy wanted to maintain this facility. "The adoption of the language in the conference report simply means that the House is making a policy decision to take the government completely out of this important undertaking, and this occurs at a time when the process shows great promise of producing the answers we have been seeking.[69] Since no other member supported Vinson's stand, the Interior Department decided to dispose of the facility on the grounds that it did not have sufficient backing to ignore the appropriations committee.[70]

On the other hand, the Atomic Energy Commission has at times disregarded nonstatutory directives when only one or two members of the influential Joint Committee on Atomic Energy stated they strongly disagreed with the appropriations committee's views. The appropriations committee, however, regulates the money supply, and thus an agency assumes a substantial risk whenever it chooses not to observe non-

68. House Hearings on Public Works Appropriations for 1958 (85-1), pp. 644-45, reprint of General Accounting Office opinion.
69. 103 *Congressional Record* 10557 (1957).
70. No money was requested in 1956 for the plant.

statutory language. This risk limits the effectiveness of floor speeches that are intended to offset nonstatutory controls. As an experienced administrator remarked: "Even if important legislators establish a substantial offsetting legislative record, it is the Appropriations Committee which can really hurt us. I must go back to the committee each year for money, not those Congressmen who made speeches on the floor."

SUMMARY

Entire House review of nonstatutory control is by no means a rare occurrence. Thus, the appropriations committee does not operate largely unchecked with regard to this important category of appropriations control.[71] The impact of a nonstatutory directive can be nullified or modified by opposition on the floor. This opposition springs from five potential protest centers within the legislative body which sometimes are mobilized by the administration. The fact that nonstatutory controls are frequently considered by the whole House provides a natural brake on an appropriations subcommittee and its chairman and mitigates possible abuses of nonstatutory devices. In short, the legislative body has repeatedly demonstrated both willingness and capacity to reject in whole or in part subcommittee proposals for nonstatutory controls.

71. It is not unusual for a subcommittee chairman to conduct part of the appropriations hearings "off the record." Nonstatutory controls that are initiated during off-the-record portions of the hearings and are not subsequently included in the subcommittee report are not subject to full committee or entire House review.

# VI.  Evaluation

At the outset of this study, three normative standards for the "proper" role of the appropriations committee were derived. Any evaluation of nonstatutory devices depends on whether extralegal controls enable the appropriations committees to better fulfill their function or whether they allow a type of control that is contrary to this proper role. Accordingly, nonstatutory techniques will be evaluated with respect to the three normative standards: appropriations control of broad policy, appropriations supervision of administrative management, and entire House review.

## NONSTATUTORY CONTROLS AND SUBSTANTIVE POLICY

Undoubtedly, nonstatutory techniques enable the appropriations committee and Congress to more effectively control broad policy than would otherwise be possible. Take for example the case of electric power wheeling agreements, where policy is determined in the process of contract negotiations between a government bureau and a non-governmental agency. In situations like this, nonstatutory devices can reconcile the need for administrative flexibility with a substantial degree of Congressional control. The appropriations committees use their reports and hearings to advance suggestions on policy that they would hesitate to legislate. Or, take the case where the appropriations committee wish to expand programs but are unable to translate their desires into specific money terms. Here they can employ nonstatutory directives that urge expansion at as fast a rate as the administrator feels is optimal. In these and many other situations nonstatutory techniques enhance the scope and depth of appropriations control over broad policy and thereby better enable the appropriations committee to fulfill one facet of their proper role.

Extralegal controls, however, are not an unmitigated blessing with respect to broad policy. Since nonstatutory language is not subject to a point of order, it is frequently employed to usurp the legislative committee's policy prerogative.[1] In fact, this characteristic of nonstatutory control is a principal reason for its use.

The proper role of the appropriations committees does not include infringement of the legislative committees' responsibility to change or add  to existing law. While the oversight efforts of the two sets of committees should overlap to some extent, it is not advantageous to have both committees proposing or modifying authorization legislation. Members of Congress are often ambivalent between economy and program development. Consequently, it would appear, they prefer that two sets of committees, each with a primary interest in one of these views, determine broad policy. Through the interaction of the different policy viewpoints, the conflicting goals of Congress will be reconciled.

With respect to new legislation, however, there is no need to have overlapping committee responsibility to reconcile the members' desires for economy and program. Since the budget document is concerned principally with the money aspects of new legislation, it is an adequate agenda for Congressional consideration of the fiscal requirements of new programs but not for consideration of legislative proposals. In short, the legislative committees should fix the broad objectives and limits of new programs, and the appropriations committees should determine the annual rate of programs based on current conditions.[2] Of course, the entire House must ratify or reject the recommendations of its committees.

1. A possible remedy for this use of nonstatutory devices will be presented in the section dealing with entire House control. If this remedy were adopted, the writer's objections to nonstatutory control of broad policy would be satisfied.

2. Through short term and even annual authorizations the legislative committees are able, if they wish, to express views and set upper limits on the current rate at which particular programs should expand.

NONSTATUTORY TECHNIQUES AND
CONTROL OF DETAILS

In Chapter I we concluded that because administrative details are necessarily related to substantive policy and economy, the appropriations committees should control administrative management. In fact, nonstatutory devices provide an important supplement to statutory regulation of executive implementation. Numerous details of personnel, procedure, procurement, and organization not suited to statutory control are regulated through hearings and reports. Also the committees frequently earmark money for specific purposes in the reports rather than the statutes. In both cases, the committees prefer extralegal techniques because they want to reconcile detailed control with administrative flexibility. Nonstatutory directives, for instance, enable an appropriations subcommittee to express i ts desire for a change in administrative procedures and organization while leaving the technical details of the change to the executive; and nonstatutory money earmarks permit legislators and administrators to adjust funds during the year if conditions change.

In effect, nonstatutory techniques expand and intensify appropriations regulation of details without the drawback of infringing to any great extent on the legislative committees' prerogative.[3] They do not represent anything qualitatively different in terms of control than statutory provisions, but instead enhance the continuity of Congressional regulation. Hence, objections to increased Congressional involvement in administration through the use of nonstatutory devices, have an insufficient foundation if they are based only on a rigid and abstract view of the separation of powers.

NONSTATUTORY TECHNIQUES AND
ENTIRE HOUSE CONTROL

The legislator's unique contribution to democratic govern-

3. Some nonstatutory directives concerned with administrative details modify or add to existing law. Such directives, however, are infrequent and of minor importance.

ment is derived from the virtues of the body as a whole, rather than from the specialized competence of its committees and subcommittees. Hence, the appropriations committees should be accountable to the whole chamber. It is significant that nonstatutory techniques to a substantial degree are subject to whole House control.

It is well known that there is relatively little time allotted to debate appropriations bills on the floor, but this applies to statutory provisions as well as nonstatutory directives.[4] As a matter of fact, it is often easier to modify nonstatutory instructions than to amend statutory language. The appropriations committee usually presents a unified opposition to most amendments, and a member who challenges the committee's recommendations often finds himself charged with something akin to rank subordination.[5] Moreover, Robert Wallace in *Congressional Control of Spending* disclosed that many members in both Houses will always support the appropriations committee, regardless of the issue.

> A large number of Members in both Houses of Congress, knowing little of the details of an issue, will side with the committee on all questions. For example, during consideration of the Defense Appropriation in 1952, Representative Vinson of Georgia took the floor to urge early House acceptance of the committee version of the bill:
> "They [the Appropriations Committee] deserve the support of every Member of this House because they are in a far better position to know the needs and necessities of national defense than you and I, who have not given it the complete and detailed study it should have."
> This was advice from the chairman of the House Armed Services Committee. . . .
> Members of Congress will hesitate to vote with a nonmember of the committee who challenges commit-

4. See speech by Representative Gross (R.-Iowa) in 108 *Congressional Record* 8223 (1962).
5. Robert Wallace, *Congressional Control of Federal Spending* (Detroit: Wayne State University Press, 1960), p. 36.

tee recommendations for fear of incurring the wrath of committee members. . . . These committee members have little patience with nonmembers who vote to upset tenuous committee compromises on amounts and question the judgement of the committee. The challenger and those supporting him are likely to find unsympathetic ears if they ever appear before the committee seeking new or increased funds for some particular object.[6]

Professor Richard Fenno contends that the main reason the appropriations committee strongly opposes most amendments is because the committee believes their sacred cow of economy will be butchered if amendments to an appropriations bill become commonplace.[7]

While it is extremely difficult to overcome the appropriations committee's opposition to an amendment, nonstatutory controls can be modified without committee acquiescence and without a majority to amend the bill. A contrary legislative record can be established by floor speeches in opposition to a committee report. Such speeches deliberately obscure the legislative history of a nonstatutory directive in order to provide the administrator with an offsetting record if he decides to disregard the committee.[8] To be successful, this method requires a bold administrator who is willing to risk committee retaliation.

Furthermore, it is probable that nonstatutory directives that raise controversial issues will be considered on the floor because of the five protest centers. Since these five protest centers cover a wide spectrum of interest and viewpoints, nonstatutory language frequently involves at least one of

6. *Ibid.*, pp. 36-87.
7. Richard Fenno, "House Appropriations Committee as a Political System," *American Political Science Review*, 56 (1962), 317.
8. Since nonstatutory directives often emerge from the nine stages of the appropriations process ambiguous and fraught with House and Senate conflicts, the administrator is able to cite offsetting legislative history if he wishes to disregard the appropriations committee. This fact mitigates the power of the appropriations committee over nonstatutory controls.

them: a constituency, a program some member is particularly interested in, the legislative committee's jurisdiction, partisan politics, or a split within an appropriations subcommittee.

It appears that the protest centers possess effective techniques to offset committee report language. A 1960 floor exchange between Senator Fulbright and several members of the Senate State Department Subcommittee illustrates the three methods by which nonmembers modify committee report language. First, Senator Fulbright established a contrary legislative history; second, he succeeded in changing the substance of the report language through a colloquy with Senator Ellender; and finally, he threatened an amendment to the conference report if other members of the subcommittee did not concur with Senator Ellender's interpretation.

> SEN. FULBRIGHT: . . . I cannot agree with the language. The language is . . . "and the [educational] exchanges with West Europe be sharply reduced." I think it would be a catastrophe to do so. I think this is the wrong interpretation of the whole objective of the program.
>
> . . . I accept that proposal if we can make the legislative history here that this is what is meant by that language. I hope the Senator from Louisiana [Sen. Ellender] will agree that he meant it to apply only to the additional money that might be granted above what is provided for the current program. . . .
>
> SEN. ELLENDER: As was pointed out by the distinguished Senator from Texas [Sen. Johnson], the amount of money provided for the 1960-61 request does not disturb the money to be allocated to Europe.
>
> ***SEN. FULBRIGHT: I am not arguing about the additional money we might receive. The language in the report was called to my attention by the State Department. They said "What does this mean? Will we be expected to live up to it?"
>
> I intended to propose to insert after the words

"Western Europe" the words "where feasible" to give them [the State Department] latitude. . . .[9]

In two respects nonstatutory devices are not subject to control by the whole House. First, an appropriations committee is able to modify existing law by writing language into a report which neither the House nor Senate can offset by an amendment. An offsetting amendment could be ruled out of order as legislation in an appropriations act. Even though contrary legislative history be sufficient to support an administrator who wishes to ignore the committee, there is no way a majority of either House can legally nullify nonstatutory controls that infringe on the legislative committee's jurisdiction.

Second, important business is transacted during meetings between subcommittee members and administrators that take place after the bill is passed. The members of the full committee and of the House and Senate are not informed of extralegal controls and reprograming that results from such informal sessions. No record is kept of the discussions, and there is no procedure for reporting to the entire body. In effect, two or three members of a subcommittee speak for the Congress. Furthermore, the subcommittee and employees of a particular bureau often use off-the-record meetings to increase the bureau's independence from central executive direction.

Such *ad hoc* sessions with executives, on the other hand, do serve a useful purpose because they enable the appropriations committees to adjust nonstatutory fund levels and other extralegal requirements to current conditions. Since nonstatutory devices permit administrative flexibility, appropriations control can be continuous and is capable of penetrating deep into administrative performance.

In sum, except for two types of situations, nonstatutory techniques fulfill the norm of entire House control. In many

9. 106 *Congressional Record* 17467-69 (1960). Note that the State Department drew the objectionable nonstatutory language to the attention of Senator Fulbright.

instances, it is easier for protestors to modify nonstatutory language than language in the bill. In the writer's opinion, since interim meetings between subcommittee members and administrators adjust nonstatutory regulations to changing conditions, they should be continued. However, formal reports to the entire legislative body should specify the results of these meetings, and in this way the subcommittee's decisions could be reviewed.[10] Of course, it is possible that the most interesting agreements would go unreported.

Several legislators and journalists have advocated that the rules of Congress permit points of order or other restrictions on appropriations committee reports.

> SEN. MCCARTHY [Minn.]: The report raises the interesting question—which should be of concern to the Senate—that, more and more, we are moving into a situation in which we have government by committee report, and sometimes the committee report is more important than the original legislation. One can make a point of order against such legislation in an appropriations bill, and perhaps we should adopt a rule which would permit us to make a point of order against such language in a committee report.[11]

If this rule were adopted, the department, recognizing that the report language represented the committees whose approval it needed for its annual budgets, might pay as much heed to that language as it does now (whether it were ruled out of order or not). Indeed, since the appropriations subcommittees would have lost none of their retaliatory powers, it seems most likely that the departments would continue to observe nonstatutory controls, and the reform would accomplish nothing.

If the departments disregarded the reports, Congress would have democratized itself only by throwing away a

10. Perhaps some time should be set aside for debate on these reports. The writer is indebted to John Berg of Harvard University for the critique of the McCarthy proposal that follows.

11. 108 *Congressional Record* 13204 (1962). See also *Washington Post*, October 30, 1963.

most effective tool of oversight. As we have seen, the value of nonstatutory controls is that they allow Congress to exercise influence in areas that are too delicate, too far outside the grasp of its own expertise, or beyond the powers of the appropriations committee to exercise absolute control. If the McCarthy reform should be adopted, the appropriations committees would lose all influence in such areas. The legislative committees, which would probably be as unwilling then as they are now to risk the enactment of strict statutory rules, would have to fall back on nonstatutory controls themselves; but they would not possess the ability to make appropriations cuts as an ultimate sanction for enforcement.

It seems unwise for Congress to surrender a technique that is so important in supervising the administration merely because the democratic norm of whole house review of that technique cannot be assured. It would be wiser to ensure that the members of the subcommittees which wield nonstatutory controls come as close as possible to representing the viewpoint of the majority of Congress.

FUTURE TRENDS

Will nonstatutory controls increase in importance and frequency in the future? Or will their use diminish and the detailed statutory limitation and proviso be revived as an oversight technique? Recent trends point to offsetting forces.

The performance budget of the early fifties, which combined numerous appropriations accounts, expanded greatly the use of nonstatutory devices. Recently, program budgets that consolidate related appropriations into more meaningful program packages are gaining increasing acceptance. Such program budgets facilitate the implementation of cost-effectiveness analyses of government programs. The Nation's defense effort, for instance, has been categorized into seven basic programs.[12] In addition, the Budget Bureau has set up a

12. See Charles J. Hitch and Roland N. McKeen, *The Economics of Defense in the Nuclear Age* (Cambridge: Harvard University Press, 1960).

special staff to help establish program budgets and cost-effectiveness analyses in all federal agencies.

Widespread installation of the program budget concept would provide a significant impetus for increased use of non-statutory strictures that could replace control through specific appropriation accounts. Consequently, the most promising type of innovation in budgeting will enhance the role of nonstatutory devices.

On the other hand, diminished importance of nonstatutory techniques may result from the legislative committee's reassertion of influence over many policy areas previously forfeited to the appropriations committees. Since World War II there has been a remarkable trend toward short-term authorizations. Indeed, over 35 per cent of the money in the President's budget for fiscal 1967 cannot be appropriated until Congress passes authorization bills that last for one year only. As we have seen, nonstatutory controls are used frequently to circumvent the rules against legislation in an appropriations act. Short-term authorizations and the consequent active exercise of oversight by the legislative committees may restrict the effective use of nonstatutory devices by appropriations committees. For instance, nonstatutory techniques could not be used as frequently to change existing law or to assert leadership in program areas that have been neglected by substantive committees.[13]

Short-term authorization has already had an impact on the common practice of reprograming funds earmarked in the reports. The Defense Department must obtain prior ap-

13. An excellent example of this trend is provided by 1965 Health Research Facilities Amendments. The legislative committee report made it clear that the reign of the appropriations committee in this area (through point of order language) was over. "Research contract authority has been available to the PHS through "point-of-order" language contained in the annual appropriation acts since FY 1957. The program of research contracts based on this temporary authority has increased steadily in size and importance ($43 million).

The reported bill would authorize the PHS to enter into contracts for research and development (or both) during FY 1966, 1967, and 1968, subject to an annual authorization ceiling of $43 million." House Report (89-247), p. 3.

proval not only from the appropriations committee but also from the Armed Services Committee before reprograming nonstatutory earmarks for aircraft, missiles, and ships.[14] In fact, short-term authorizations appear to be increasing the use of nonstatutory controls by legislative committees and extending substantive committee influence over nonstatutory devices employed by appropriations committees.

At this time there are no indications that statutory proviso will become an increasingly important oversight technique. Indeed, interviews with appropriations committee members and staff reveal a strong predilection in favor of administrative flexibility through nonstatutory devices—provided this flexibility is not exercised without informing Congress. Consequently, it is probable that the future of nonstatutory techniques depends on the balance of the opposing trends outlined above, rather than a renewed Congressional preference for statutory limitations.

One future trend appears certain. The role of Congress as an oversight body will continue to grow as policy initiation is left increasingly to the executive branch. Consequently, nonstatutory controls will play an important part in enhancing the oversight effectiveness of both legislative and appropriations committees.

14. See House Hearings on Defense Appropriations for 1961 (87-1), pp. 172-74.

# Index

## A

Administrative details, control by appropriations committees, 18-20, 155

Administrative reorganization, 38, 88-89

Agriculture, Department of, 5, 28, 34, 36, 37, 42, 46, 49, 60, 80, 109, 117, 125-26, 134, 142, 147, 148

Appropriations committee staff, functions, 9; role in drafting report, 122-25 *passim*

Appropriations hearings, description, 6; used for control of executive policy, 23-30, 65; verbal commitments, 26, 27, 28; review of agency implementation, 65, 74

Area Redevelopment Administration, 52-53

Army Corps of Engineers, 19, 27, 44, 58, 60, 94, 95, 98, 101, 117, 130

Atomic Energy Commission, 26, 81-82, 105, 151, 69-70

Authorization committees, 13-17, 84-88 *passim*, 119, 121, 141, 154, 162

## B

Banfield, Edward, 18

Banking and Currency Committee, 11

Broad policy, influence of appropriations committees, 11-17; evaluation of nonstatutory controls, 153-55

Bureau of the Budget, 79-81, 90, 110, 135, 137, 161

Bureau of Mines, 111

Bureau of Reclamation, 33, 37, 62, 68, 76, 145

## C

Carrol, Holbert, 116, 121

Committee mark-up, 123-28 *passim*

Committee reports, description, 6; technique for nonstatutory control, 30-39; effectiveness of control, 68; procedures for drafting, 122-28 *passim*

Commodity Credit Corporation, 5, 74-75, 120, 142, 148

Conference reports, use for nonstatutory control, 50-58; statement of managers, 51-52; compromises on nonstatutory language, 53-55; floor debate, 57

Congressional investigations, 74

Congressional Reorganization Act of 1946, 15

Continuous oversight, explanation, 8-10; adjustments in nonstatutory controls, 129, 138, 159

Cooper, Joseph, 15

## D

Debakey, Michael, 92, 132-34

Defense, Department of, 4, 83-84, 91-92, 106, 108, 163

Dixon-Yates power project, 48, 127

## F

Farber, Sidney, 92, 132-34

Federal budget, 15, 154

Federal contract negotiations, 54-55, 103, 153

Federal Flood Control Act, 12

Fenno, Richard, study of appropriations committee norms, 13, 21, 127; analysis of appropriation procedure, 57, 64, 143, 157

Sharkansky, Ira, 79
Soil Conservation Service, 25, 101
Southwest Power Administration, 49-50, 59-60, 150
Specification of purpose, description, 4-5; as a sanction 77-78
State, Department of, 35, 40, 43-44, 69, 93, 101, 114-15, 144
Subcommittee chairman, powers 11, 138-39; role in drafting report, 122-28 *passim*; interim adjustment of appropriation, 129
Supreme Court, 6-7

T

Tennessee Valley Authority, 81, 112
Thomas, Morgan, 26

U

United States Forest Service, 90, 132-34
United States Information agency, 40, 70-71, 93
Upper Colorado Power Transmission, 54-55, 127

V

Voluntary organizations. *See* Pressure groups

W

Wallace, Robert, 156
Ways and Means Committee, 3
Wilmerding, Lucius, 113

www.ingramcontent.com/pod-product-compliance
Lightning Source LLC
Chambersburg PA
CBHW030652270326
41929CB00007B/321